Staying Alive:
A Love Story

Laura B. Hayden

Staying Alive: A Love Story
by Laura B. Hayden

Signalman Publishing 2011
www.signalmanpublishing.com
email: info@signalmanpublishing.com
Kissimmee, Florida

Cover design by: Dale Ulrich

The article *Rare Case of Dementia Leaves Woman Speechless* by
Peter Gott, M.D., reprinted with permission.

Photo on back cover by Guardrail Photography

ISBN: 978-1-935991-18-2

Library of Congress Control Number: 2011937066

To Larry and our children, Emily and Conor, with love.

CONTENTS

FOREWORD

Staying Alive: A Love Story is a story of hope and renewal that centers on a woman's search for meaning after the untimely death of her 49-year-old husband. Coupled with other experiences of loss in her life, she is determined to, with her children, persevere.

Like Annie Dillard, Hayden draws on the rhythms and rituals of the natural world to explore her Brooklyn roots and New England adulthood. Wild creatures and domesticated critters, seasides and hillsides, proffer comfort and understanding as she comes to realize that "no more than a hairline and no less than an eternity" separate her from the man she loved. Even with the wear and tear her faith endures, it rarely diminishes.

Her purpose – to usher her two grieving children through a difficult adolescence to a well-adjusted adulthood – resonates through her own struggles. With the precise objectivity reminiscent of Joan Didion's *The Year of Magical Thinking* and Joyce Carol Oates' *A Widow's Story*, Hayden recounts the day her husband died and the rituals and obsessions of the bereaved. Forced to look at death straight in the eye, the author stares back, wide-eyed, without blinking through her tears.

Hayden also manages to be seriously droll - in an Anne Lamott way. Never is her humor more honed than in the portrayal of her deceased spouse, whose devotion, antics, and wisdom remain ever-present to those who are staying alive without him. His death becomes not only the family's heartbreak, but the loss of a well-executed life for all who knew him or will get to know him through these essays.

Whether Laura Hayden's writing deals with herself, her children, or her cadre of loved ones, it is clear that she, her daughter, and her son emerge from their tragic loss survivors, not victims of Larry's death, an outcome of which he would be very pleased. In a culture of intentionally exposed and celebrated self-victimization, the story of this family may be considered a quiet triumph.

John McClure
Publisher

ACKNOWLEDGMENTS

Staying Alive: A Love Story would remain a figment of my imagination without the encouragement of my early advisors in the Western Connecticut State University MFA in Creative and Professional Writing program: Irene Sherlock, Daniel Asa Rose, J.D. Scrimgeour, and Brian Clements, director of the program. Peers in my Online Multigenre Workshops, along with facilitators, Brian Clements, Victoria Ludwin, Oscar De Los Santos, and Holly Azevedo, offered continual assistance and support. WCSU Residency Workshops conducted by Elizabeth Cohen and Steve Almond also impacted the manuscript.

I am especially grateful for my thesis advisors, Mark Sundeen and Daniel Nester, masterful writers and mentors. Thanks also go to John McClure at Signalman Publishing and Dale Ulrich at owls. com.

LOSING

Larry was the first to spot the three dolphins moving parallel to a shoreline under the dry California sun. One of the dolphins seemed to lead the slow progress of the other two. Another nudged the third through the rippling waters with its head. The dolphin being pushed floated dorsal side up. It soon became clear that the upturned dolphin was dead.

This behavior was no quirk for the bottlenose dolphin. A *Reuters* piece tells the story about a dolphin that worked for hours in a busy Florida waterway to revive her dead calf. "She pushed the calf and would come up beneath her, trying to get her to move," said a female worker at a bait shop on the bank of the Alafia River. Another eyewitness reported the dolphin "wouldn't let anyone get near the calf." Bottlenose dolphins often spend two or three days mourning their dead before abandoning them.

We stood frozen on the edge of the water that day. The procession moved so slowly that hours later, when we were back in our car, driving no more than a mile or so up Canyon Hills Highway, we caught sight of the salt-water entourage again as it continued steadily up the Pacific to who knows where.

Four months later, Emily, Conor, and I escorted our Larry to his grave.

I awake in the well of the family room sofa bed mattress, curled in a loose fetal position, listing into Larry's right arm. He lies on his back still unable to turn to his side, two weeks after heart surgery. Still unable to climb the stairs to our bedroom on the second floor.

"Morning," he says, glancing down at me as I start to unfurl.

"Morning," I repeat, moving my arm across his waist for a moment. I am careful not to touch the zipper-like stitching stretched lengthwise across his sternum.

"Getting there," I say. I start to rise to my knees and arch my body over him to avoid putting any pressure on his chest. We kiss. A mutual smack on the lips we could not maneuver in bed a day ago.

"Getting there," he repeats.

I step out of bed and move to the bottom of the mattress to put knee-high elastic stockings over his feet and legs. He wears these to aid his circulation and prevent blood clots. He rests awhile, as I get the children off to school.

"Dad's awake. You can go say good-bye to him before the bus comes," I tell them before they leave.

When they are gone I return to help Larry get up to take his walk. Movement is another clotting deterrent. I do not go off to my high school teaching job. I am on a family medical leave to take care of my husband.

Three weeks earlier I received a call at the high school where I teach English.

"They're sending me to the hospital," I heard Larry say on the school secretary's office phone. It was a Friday afternoon. The night before, we had attended Parents Night at Emily's middle school. Larry had an appointment for a stress test the next day. He had been taking a daily aspirin since his annual fall physical a few weeks earlier, when he complained about tiredness.

Three months earlier, on our California visit to Larry's brother's family, we stopped at a steep sand dune. Everyone except Larry chose to walk up and down the challenging slope. Uncharacteristically, he said he was too tired.

As a follow-up to his regular physical that included an EKG, the doctor ordered Larry to start taking the aspirin and made him an appointment for a stress test a week later. Larry downplayed the test, even though his father had died of a heart attack a few months earlier. Brought his business clothes to the appointment with him, so he could scoot to work afterward.

Instead of going to work afterward, he called me.

"They're ordering me not to drive." His voice was shaky.

I headed straight to the testing site. We left his car parked in the lot and drove to the hospital in mine. He was admitted on the results of the stress test.

That soon, the village in which all caring humankind resides began to assist us through the crisis of our lives. I called the mother of Conor's sixth-grade classmate. She agreed to bring Conor home with her after school - for an unplanned visit. I arranged to have Meme, Larry's mother, at the house for when Em got back from her field trip to the Statue of Liberty later in the afternoon. When Conor returned home, Meme brought the children to her house – two miles up Town Farm Road – for dinner and an overnight stay. I spent the night in a recliner in Larry's hospital room.

We were a family still in shock over Larry's father's death six months earlier. Meme had returned home from an afternoon errand and found him lying in the yard, too late. Struck by a heart attack while mowing the lawn, the day before they were to leave on a family vacation to Florida with their youngest son's family.

Larry, the hospital doctors told us less than a week before Thanksgiving, had not had a heart attack. The stress test detected an extremely high risk for one. So high that he was ordered to hospital monitoring until more tests could be administered on Monday morning.

The children visited him on the weekend.

"I'm here so the doctors can prevent what happened to Gramps," he told them. Larry played the in-house educational channel on the hospital room TV, a heavy box that was shelved close to the ceiling in the corner of his single-patient quarters. A bright yellow helium balloon the children brought floated below the TV, weighted to the floor and decorated with the simple black markings of a smiley face. Already, a get well card from his sister and a plant from co-workers were propped on a table by the window. Tacked onto a small bulletin board on the wall across from his bed was a drawing of a monkey sent by a neighbor's son. Above the primate's head "Feel Better

Coach Hayden" appeared in an eight-year-old's deliberate penmanship.

We all tilted our heads upward to watch videos on coronary heart disease that illustrated how blocked arteries impede a healthy blood flow to an overworked heart. The children saw how, with an angiogram, an X-ray can locate blocked blood vessels after the patient is injected with dye; how, with an angioplasty, the doctor can guide a tiny collapsed balloon through a blood vessel from a small incision in the patient's groin to the blocked artery - and inflate it to unclog the blood vessel. Then the doctor on the screen directed a collapsed metal stent (smaller and flatter than a ball point pen spring) to the spot. We watched a blown-up animation of the stent expanding and securing itself to prevent the artery from closing up again. The viewing had a Bill-Nye-the-Science-Guy feel to it.

Larry's angioplasty early Monday morning detected four clogged arteries – too many for the noninvasive fix. That afternoon we viewed the more daunting video on coronary by-pass surgery: Learned how a blood vessel would be taken from his leg and grafted to his coronary arteries to improve the blood supply to his heart – bypassing the clogged vessels – and how the heart would be stopped and started again during the operation. Larry said knowing helped understanding. Understanding lessened fear - for all of us. Teachable moments before two doctors entered with details of the surgery to be performed early the next morning.

"Your heart's strong. No damage," said one doctor.

"This should be a breeze for a fit 49-year-old like you," said the other, in front of the children.

Larry had quadruple by-pass surgery the day before Thanksgiving. I visited him in CICU a few hours afterward, walked up to his body monitored by tubes, IVs, and breathing apparatus. He could only manage two gestures. The rise of a single eyebrow – an ability his children have inherited – indicated he recognized me. Then his hand moved, forming a single thumbs up.

After the children leave for school I help Larry out of bed. It has been a week since his week-long stay in the hospital, fourteen days since surgery. His recovery seems slow but steady. Today he will visit a doctor for the first time since returning home. His mother, a retired nurse, will join us.

He walks up and down the hallway and through the dining room, family room, and kitchen, an indoor course he has mapped and repeated more often every day, as I start the shower. I've propped an outdoor chair in the tub so he can sit under the spray.

Meme arrives when he is in his bathrobe. She gives him a prayer card she has picked up at church that morning - December 8, in honor of the Feast of the Immaculate Conception.

As I help Larry dress in loose sweatpants, a roomy buttoned shirt and fleece zippered vest, he rubs the back of his knee joint. Says it feels a little stiff. Bends the joint back and forth a few times. Says he is fine. Ready to go. He walks to the family room to rejoin his mother. I go to grab the car keys, my list of questions for the doctor, his coat, and then head to the family room that opens to the garage. But I never get that far.

Larry is breathing rapidly, too rapidly, as his mother lowers him into a soft swivel rocker. His face has lost its morning shower glow. It looks grayish - and scared. He looks at me and says "Call the doctor."

I leave him with his mother, run to the phone, but call 911 instead. "Something's gone wrong. He's two weeks post op and we are on our way to the doctor, but he's gasping for air." When I return Meme stands helpless and Larry is slumped in the soft chair. I shout his name, tap his cheek. "Larry, Larry can you hear me?" I am slapping his face now, hitting him hard. So hard the swivel chair turns to the left.

The paramedics arrive, almost momentarily it seems, and never stop moving. I am relegated into the kitchen shouting, *"He just had bypass surgery,"* but I can hear that this is no time for a light touch, for the gentleness with which I hugged him just two hours earlier. I hear what I think is chest thumping. I cringe and go to his mother who is in the dining room. We are in each other's arms. I pray to the Holy Mother: *despise not my petition but hear and answer me.* "No, no, not again," Meme repeats over and over. She doesn't even realize when I slip away. I know I must get to the phone to call my sister-in-law at work in the high school cafeteria.

"Linda, something's wrong and Meme's here. I'm going with the ambulance." Linda asks no questions. I can picture her tearing off her apron and heading to the exit as she utters just four syllables, "I'm on my way."

In the ambulance on the way to the hospital I scream from the passenger seat, "Larry, can you hear me. Don't leave us. Please God, don't let him leave us."

I turn to the driver. "Can he hear me?" I ask.

"Yes, he can," he says.

I continue to shout.

At the hospital I am led to an admitting desk and then some sort of crisis waiting room with the hospital chaplain. I ask him to call Father Kerwan, our parish priest, to tell him to go to my mother who would not be able to bear any sort of bad news alone. I know my sister-in-law will take care of the rest of the family - and she does; for she, her husband, and Meme enter the room just before the doctor comes in. Just before he starts to say, "We did everything we could. . ."

MISSING

I have come to realize I took my 20 years together with Larry for granted. Larry didn't. Perhaps it was because he had married his college sweetheart – just after graduation in 1972 – and divorced five years later. When we wed, in 1980, Larry embraced our marriage the way a once - starved man comes to appreciate regular meals. The shadow of his divorce gradually faded into the background of our lives.

The late Senator Ted Kennedy has spoken publically about his second wife Victoria, how she *re*awakened in him feelings and emotions that "had been banked" after his failed marriage to Joan. The chaos brought about by the deaths of his four siblings – along with his own divorce – spurred him to value his relationship with Victoria more than he would have been able to as a younger man. The same was true of Larry.

At work at the Connecticut Labor Department, Larry understood the pain his unemployment clients felt after losing their jobs in the Eighties recession. He had once stood in a Norwalk unemployment line himself, a recipient of benefits. A few years later, as a State employee, he led the Rapid Response Team directly to job sites– to companies like Hamilton Standard, Pratt & Whitney, Pitney Bowes - employers that once offered their workers a lifetime of security. He assisted the jobless clients even before they left their workplace for the last time, when they were still caught up in the shock of their job loss. Larry took them, step-by-step, through paperwork that would start their benefits. On weekends, on his own time, he began an unemployment support group at our church.

"I don't know what I would have done if he didn't hold my hand through the process," a teacher, who had been laid-off in 1985, recently reminded me - well over ten years after Larry's death. The losses of his past fueled his empathy and intensified his sense of purpose.

Though I cherished my relationship with my husband Larry, I could never compete with the scope of his devotion for me. Only since his death have I come to fully appreciate his love, his humor, his compassion. I wish now that I had laughed harder at his everyday delights. I wish I hadn't rolled my eyes so much whenever he told the peanut butter toast story – a tale often repeated among family and friends. I was always a little embarrassed about how it made me look. Him, just opening the Sunday paper, casually mentioning how, as a kid, he use to like peanut butter toast; me, newly married, wanting to please.

I quietly slip into the kitchen to find a peanut butter bread recipe in my Fannie Farmer cookbook. In minutes I beat eggs, flour, sugar, and peanut butter in a bowl. Pour the thick batter into a loaf pan and pop it in the oven. Fifty minutes at 375 degrees. I return to Larry and the Sunday *Home* section.

Halfway through the baking time Larry puts down the morning news: predictions of Reagan's win over Carter, more executions in Tehran, and a Sox win over the Athletics in the bottom of the tenth.

"How 'bout breakfast?" he asks.

"It'll be ready in about forty-five minutes," I say. I figure the bread will take a half hour more in the oven, then five or ten minutes cooling in the pan before I could pop it out and gingerly slice a few pieces - still warm. Then I'd be able to drizzle a little butter and put the breakfast bread under the broiler for a quick browning.

"How long does it take to toast a couple of slices of bread and spread peanut butter on them?" he asks.

"Ohhh. *That's* peanut butter toast?" I say.

He never tired of telling the tale of my naïve devotion. How I wish I could hear him tell it again.

If, immediately after losing Larry, I was able to center my attention more on life, rather than death, I would have recalled then, as I do now – ten years later – the levity he infused into our lives. The look of his outstretched arms and animated face, for instance, when he'd return from his office at the Labor Department to announce, "I'm on *VACATION*," whenever our week on Martha's Vineyard lay ahead. Larry could turn the mundane merry. Family members will never forget his tongue-twisting contract – he called it *A Legalese Legal Lease (L^3)* – written to his skeptical parents when he borrowed their Christmas tree a few years back.

> The heart, soul, thrust, point, gist, and intent of said agreement (hereafter referred to as "The Fleecing,") is to loan one slightly used and verbally abused – but functionally decorative – counterfeit Yuletide kindling (hereafter referred to as "The Ersatz Evergreen" or "E^2") to said scion for seasonal use. Said E^2 will be promptly returned by aforementioned offspring in the last week of the third month in the Year of the Kinkajou.

Larry could make any occasion festive – he liked that word *festive* – and he looked for ways to add its touch to events like the Patriots Super Bowl in '97. WDRC -FM aired his spirited rally for the New England team which he wrote and sang to the tune of *The Battle of New Orleans.* If only I could recall its every word. If only I could have focused on his life with us instead of spin in the vortex of his unexpected death in '98.

There are still days when I cannot escape the force pulling me back to the day, the hour, the precise wretched minute when a blood clot dislodged from his lower leg where an artery had been removed, fourteen days earlier. The artery, replanted, became a bypass route for clogged vessels near his heart. A successful, miraculous surgery gone awry, two weeks to the day after the operation, four months to the day after we saw the dolphins in Canyon Hills.

That was when the rogue wave of Larry's sudden death first overtook me.

Caught in its undertow of grief, I tossed to and fro between drowning and surfacing for air.

Until a tow line – my children – pulled me back to shore.

In the few weeks between playing Mrs. Scrooge in her eighth-grade Christmas play and agreeing to "go out with" her first middle-school beau, my daughter Emily lost her father. It is no surprise to me that Emily, now in her mid-twenties, still measures the wit and wisdom of the young man committed to her well-being today, by the high standard set by her Dad.

In the early morning before Larry's death, Conor left for school excited about the singing solo he would rehearse for his sixth-grade holiday show coming up in a week. Well over ten years later I see Larry's height, thick curly hair, and chiseled features in Conor, now 23. I hear Larry's voice in Conor's sports blog and signature closing:

"As always, stay tuned and stay sassy."

I often think of how my children have endured since the most terrible day of their lives. And whenever I do, the statement echoes back to me in the form of a question: How have my children endured since the most terrible day of their lives?

We all had to endure the same public school ritual where I was asked to convey, in person, the tragic news that their father had died. At both schools I spoke in the presence of principals, teachers, and school nurses. The librarian at Emily's middle school picked me up at home and comforted me through our walk to the Health Suite, where Emily waited.

"I need to tell you that your father loved you more than his own life," I began. I remember the words were, oddly, not difficult to find. They seemed cruelly obvious to me. I slowly continued. "But something very bad happened today after you left for school."

Emily's body tightened. *How bad,* her wide frozen stare conveyed.

"Very bad," I said, struggling to keep my composure. "Daddy died, honey," I told her.

Emily collapsed like a tower of ash into my arms. I said again how her father loved her more than his own life. Supportive adults surrounded us for some time. Then we were driven home, where Emily stayed with her shocked grandmothers. Her aunt and uncle drove me to Conor's school. Neither of them left my side until Conor and I returned home.

Upon my arrival to the grammar school, Conor was gently pulled out of his sixth-grade holiday show rehearsal and brought to the principal's office, assured that he was not in any kind of trouble.

I began the same as I had with Emily. When I got to "Daddy died," I tried hard to subdue my sobs, but an involuntary caving within my chest turned my attempt to speak into a series of coughing gasps. I tried hard to catch my breath. I curbed one spasm long enough to say, "But I know your father loved the life he had with us." I hoped that both my children could in some way comprehend the rest, as I purposely continued. "And he would want you to know that he died loving you more than anything in the world."

At the time I didn't know exactly from where these words came. I have come to believe that they emerged from deep within a core a grieving mother instinctively discovers, coming to understand this: that even despair is no excuse to mistakenly measure her sorrow more important than her children's heartache. I think back now, as I even did then, to another Kennedy family story, a behind-the scenes account of President Kennedy's funeral which revealed Jackie tending to the details of her son John-John's third birthday party, celebrated the same day as her husband's funeral.

I might just as well have siphoned the air out of Conor's lungs as I spoke to him within the walls of his principal's office. I watched him deflate before my eyes, fall into my arms. He clutched me so tightly, his legs wrapped around my torso, squeezing me against the back of the chair. As he sobbed inconsolably into my right shoulder, I too, could barely breathe. And then, on the car ride through a cold and rainy stretch back to Emily and the family members who waited at home, Conor silently brought his finger to the lightly fogged car window and slowly drew a circle. He dotted two eyes within it and then placed a frown on the very un-smiley face. After staring at it a moment he turned to say, "I guess Christmas just won't be as festive this year," his voice steadier than at school.

HARBINGER

An unexpected event occurred on the way from the funeral home to Larry's service. The long and slow procession came to a halt on both sides of the four-way stop signs, 500 feet from Holy Family Church. The hearse that carried Larry's casket had crossed the intersection and stopped. My limo, which also transported the children, Larry's mother, and my mother, waited on the other side. Even now, thousands of days after his death, I retreat back to that moment as if it were yesterday.

I see, frozen in time, a golden-hued dog that appears out of the blue, no owner in sight, on the corner of Simon and Post Office Roads. I watch the dog cross into the road to set himself behind Larry's hearse. It begins to walk back and forth as if guarding the vehicle's contents, at the same time looking straight at me, its head held high.

"Look at that dog," I say. The dog paces across the tailgate around to just where the casket lies.

The dog doesn't leave the territory he's staked out for himself in front of our car and behind the hearse. Three or four minutes go by. The funeral director and chauffeur make final decisions before driving the one-tenth mile stretch up Simon Road to the church parking lot. And as soon as the procession moves, this unescorted creature rises and starts to follow the rear of the casket-bearing limousine. The dog follows the front of the chain of vehicles - around the back lot to the front entrance of Holy Family. The limousine parks behind Larry's hearse. We watch the pallbearers pull and lift the casket out.

The dog sits on the front steps of the church, its eyes transfixed on the casket's movement up from vehicle to vestibule.

Whether its presence is divine or divined through the gaze of my grief, the dog vanishes by the time the funeral procession brings us back out to the hearse. The dog's disappearance is reason enough for me to drop any delusion that acts in this everyday world will become more fully and clearly understood in some other time or place. I let go of any notion of a connection between Larry's spirit and the commanding dog - until a second, oddly comforting event occurs at the start of his funeral mass.

As Emily, Conor, and I take our places behind the casket to begin the procession down the Holy Family aisle, one of the church deacons on the altar catches my eye and flashes me a thumbs up. A common enough sign of support, I suppose. But standing in a church aisle beside my husband's body– the same aisle Larry and I walked just short of twenty years earlier – I seek more meaning. I think of resurrection, a Christian belief. When I was ten, preparing for my Confirmation, the *Baltimore Catechism* drilled one, of many, questions and answers into my head:

> In what state will the bodies of the just rise?
> The bodies of the just will rise, glorious and immortal.

I take the heavenward motion of the deacon's hand as a confirmation of resurrection on this, the third day after Larry's death. The gesture also brings back the memory of Larry, two weeks earlier, in the CICU, six or seven hours after his quadruple bypass. When he signaled the thumbs up to me, the same gesture I see just before processing the body to the altar.

I make the connection to Larry's hospital bedside as soon as the deacon's hand rises. But the presence of the dog through the funeral procession and the dolphin retinue in California four months ago do not start to resonate until after my experience with a bird, in the spring.

The children and I are camping with in-laws and cousins on Memorial Day weekend, late Saturday or Sunday afternoon. It is unusually quiet during the hour lull after swimming and before lighting the campfire for dinner, except for the oldies station playing on the radio by the tent. The girls have fallen asleep; the boys are on the bocce court, and my head nods as I slip back and forth between reality and reverie. I am drawn to a tiny commotion in a pine treetop. I follow the flash of red spiraling downward until a fiery crimson male cardinal lands by my chair. He hops and directs his chatter toward me, shifting his head from side to side as if to emphasize a point. Then another flash occurs – this one from the past – as "Ooh Child," a crossover tune from the Seventies, plays its lyric about how "things are gonna get easier" and someday being able "to walk in the rays of a beautiful sun." As the cardinal continues to twist its head to and fro at me, I remember how Larry would turn this tune up on the car radio, telling the kids to *quiet down* because it was *Mom's song*. At that moment I realize there is no more than a hairline and no less than an eternity between him and me.

Is it so surprising that after the camping trip, I became more attuned to my yard birds, not to mention a particularly large and luminescent Luna moth that clung to a nearby window on the night of Emily's eighth-grade graduation dance? The iridescent insect spread six inches across the height and width of the window, as if it longed to join us, but, unable to get past the screen, settled for keeping an eye on the young teen party inside. Looking like a shimmering alien, it clung to the fine wire mesh, the only barrier separating its reality from the world of Emily's emerging womanhood, so captured in the feminine flow of her sage semi-formal and accented by the fresh orchid in her hair.

As I write this sentence, still unsure, after years, of what to make of these series of events, I see a male cardinal perched on a bare lilac branch out back, his characteristic screech drawing my attention from laptop to his welcome nod. I take it as a cue that I have said enough, for now, on the matters of life after Larry's death. I turn, instead, to memories of our days together.

NESTING

L arry and I first moved into our fixer-upper in 1981, the year after we married. We made sure we bought a house we could afford on one salary, so I could leave my teaching job for a few years and stay home with the baby we hoped to have. As we moved in our living room furniture, a mourning dove slammed into the front bay window. It left feathers on a moist, pinkish splotch on the glass. I recoiled at the notion that a dead bird lay on the ground on the other side of the glass. After an hour or so, I went out to remove it and its mark on the window. The bird was gone. It must have only stunned itself on impact, revived, and flown away.

Over those first few weeks, the pine tree in front of the picture window filled with chickadees, cardinals, tufted titmice, and an occasional woodpecker. Serenaded by their birdsong every day, I grew accustomed to the occasional bump, collision, and resurrection of a bird as, once again, one mistook its reflection in the pane for another bird and flew into the glass to greet it.

Larry and I had been trying to start a family for three years, but nothing was happening. In the midst of having begun fertility counseling, Larry suggested, "We should get a puppy." We had been in our new home for only two months.

I looked around at our house's chipped and faded exterior, worn rugs, and pink and black tile bathroom. House-hunting had confirmed my suspicion that all 25-year-old houses had pink-and-black tile bathrooms. But we had bought the house, like so many other things, for its promise, not its polish. A bit of painting inside now and pruning outside, in the spring, and we'd be well on our way to turning the needy, mid-fifties ranch into a rather pleasant home. With its fenced-in yard, it was already perfect for a dog.

"Well," I said, "It'll mean getting up earlier, leaving it alone during the day, and staying close to home most weekends." *No* is a word not often used by a wife who revered, even envied, a husband's spontaneity. But I had to be realistic, play Mrs. Panza to my Mr. Quixote. Plus, I knew if the social restraint did not dissuade Larry, nothing would. I ended with the frequent plaint of the working wife. "I can't do it all."

"You won't."

I thought getting a dog meant going to the pound for a homeless pup. Larry had other plans. This was to be a long-term commitment. He said type and temperament were of the utmost importance. A call to Nutmeg Dog Breeder Referral supplied us with the phone number of a West Highland White Terrier breeder twenty minutes away. Larry phoned the Gingerbread Kennels and we were invited to see the pregnant pedigree, Jeanne, and her breeder Judy.

I wondered about a dog with a person's name, but when Jeanne greeted us at the kennels, she was as licking, gnawing, and sniffing a terrier as she could be. Toto incarnate.

Judy the breeder greeted us with less fervor than Jeanne, but still warmly. A sweet face supported her thick glasses. Along with a pleasantly thick body, this made her appear to be the human facsimile of a thoughtful mongrel that would be easy to love. Amiable Judy, however, turned quickly staid over the business of choosing a home for one of Jeanne's impending pups.

No one doubted that, as Judy stated, Jeanne would be a mother on May seventh. She had mated in March. With dogs, fertilization was pretty much a sure bet. Sixty-three days later Jeanne would give birth to, most likely, four pups. Thoughts of my own temperature charts, insidious infertility tests, and disappointing counseling sessions crossed my mind. I began to wish my name was Lassie instead of Laura. Maybe canine breeding odds would rub off on me.

"So you want a Westie?" Judy stared at me. Since I knew nothing about dogs I worked on camouflaging my cluelessness by tossing my head, relaying the stare and the question to Larry.

"Oh yes. I want a dog that enjoys people, is an exuberant welcomer, an intelligent learner." Judy smiled. Larry knew what he was talking about. He continued. "Had a Scottie once. . . Merlin." Larry paused, looking almost wistful. "Merlin was fun," he paused again, "but I've always liked the personality of a Westie."

Judy's body language indicated she was satisfied with Larry's knowledge of Westies, but I hadn't passed the ownership test yet. She shot the next question directly at me. "So you know terriers too?"

"Ah, well." I hesitated. "Larry does. I, err, you see, never had a dog. But Larry's grown up with them."

"I see," said Judy. "And where do you live?"

This was beginning to sound like an adoption screening. Larry quickly answered, "We just bought a home – with a great yard. Over half an acre."

Judy looked reasonably pleased. I summoned the confidence to add, "A fenced-in yard."

Her eyeglasses slightly magnified her widening eyes. "The entire half-acre?"

"Chain-linked," I said.

"Well then," she clucked like a mother hen. "The litter will be here in early May. I'll put your name on the list and call you then."

Larry put out his hand. "Thank you, Jeanne."

"I'm Judy," she said, shaking on the done deal.

Three months later we brought our tiny Westie home. Piper's days filled with short spurts of puppy craziness and long naps. Like our home, he was needy. We ministered to first-night frights, encouraged his little body over steps, placed heartworm medicine down his throat, and rubbed, often, his wanting belly. If a puppy is, like a man, what he eats, Piper – named for the player of Scottish pipes – fit his portion of eight parts dry Puppy Chow to one part canned Mighty Dog.

As weeks passed, the Mighty Dog share of the canine concoction increased. I grew more and more uncomfortable with the smell of greater portions of moist, meaty byproducts mixed with the less pungent pellets. Before long, a mere whiff of the dog's food nauseated me - which thrilled me! I made a special trip to the corner drug store – a long-time family business that use to give out free sundaes for good grades when I was in grammar school – and bought a pregnancy test. Actually, I bought three pregnancy tests, and within an hour *FACT. The home pregnancy test that gives the fastest possible results* confirmed I was expecting, once, twice, and then a third time. I called Larry when I was sure.

"Guess what?"

"The Coleco stock finally rebounded," he said, one of his many attempts to make light of his investment, gone sour, months earlier.

"Better," I said.

"Reeeaally?" There were almost three syllables in his exaggerated articulation.

"Reeeaally." I imitated his emphasis. "We're having a baby."

We celebrated that night, clinking chilled Perrier in crystal goblets. I just glowed.

There must have been a range of two octaves between Piper's high, excited yips as the vet calmly administered four vaccinations and the guttural tones the puppy directed to the tabby in the waiting room. "Good timing," said our friendly veterinarian, herself heavy with child. "A puppy in July, a baby in March," continued the vet. "If you keep him out of the nursery now, he won't resent the baby later."

It was difficult to imagine Piper resenting anything. Even when we scolded him with a stern "No," he would lurk by our heels like a repentant sinner. He liked to wrestle with the give-and-take of leather shoes - another no-no. Sometimes he would roll on his back and gnaw a rawhide chew as if he was a floating otter enjoying a precious piece of abalone. Each week Piper napped less and played more, the way a baby would, I thought. Now and then the thump of a misguided mourning dove on window glass drove him to a barking frenzy.

And he did stay out of our baby's waiting room, never looking as if he really understood why the "No," by the nursery-in-waiting was so emphatic.

A misguided mourning dove smudges a window. A puppy accident on a rug. These became the least of my concerns.

I was spotting.

Bright red stains on my summer shorts interrupted our bliss. Doctors and medical books offered no remedies for symptoms that indicated my baby was about to slip away. Instead, they gave odds: a fifty-fifty chance that the pregnancy would miscarry. The books stated a lost fetus is a sick fetus. A sick fetus would continue to develop into an abnormal baby. Most often, a miscarriage eliminates a fetus that would not have lived very long if brought to term.

My doctor ordered bed rest. We would have to wait and see if our baby would survive the sign of internal stress.

Larry took on the kitchen duties. He served his first meals with panache and flair. Fat tomatoes from the garden stuffed with cold chunks of white tuna, our own squash steamed to a still-crisp perfection, and the windowsill parsley garnishing it all. By week's end Larry would be heating frozen dinners.

"I'm tired," he said.

"I know," I would reassure him, as we traded our private ironies: Larry, the weary, working house-husband; me, exhausted, from bedrest and worry. At night we hugged hard, as if hoping the tight embrace would keep our baby intact. Piper slept under our bed.

A trace of blood appeared on the sheets.

In a few days Larry opened the door to the nursery that, after the miscarriage, reverted back to spare room status. Piper frantically sniffed at its threshold and then curiously peered. The variegated rug, as thick as his double-coated fur, contrasted with the flat pile of the worn hallway rug. A bright latch-hook hanging of a koala bear caught the attention of his black eyes. He did not enter, but moved his hind legs in a bicycling motion while his forelegs remained stiff and still. We heard an almost imperceptible growl.

"Good dog," I said, bending down and patting him.

Through the next few weeks our daily routine lacked meaning and momentum. Larry and I no longer talked of cribs and changing tables. We didn't compare canary yellow paint samples to goldenrod. The neutral ecru tint on the wall in the empty room would do.

Conversation remained in the present, avoiding the immediate past and any hopes for a future that would include a child. Larry went to work. I would have to wallow in more worrisome places at home, with the dog, until my teaching job restarted after Labor Day. Though my body had healed after my miscarriage, the mind still oozed. I felt empty. I felt robbed.

One late August morning I was about to let Piper out into the dewy yard as I did every morning. Tall, thick pines, like the one outside the front bay window, lined the inside of its chain-linked perimeter. Piper must have thought these trees were, truly, the boundaries of the world. He took his customary, slow hop down the step. But, today, his usual sleepy walk halted. Ears up, snout frozen, Piper heard first, what I heard next.

A robin's sound.

My puppy hurled into a blurry, barking streak at the bird in the grass. This would not have been an unusual scene, except that the robin did not fly away. And quicker than I could throw balls, bones, anything to distract Piper from this creature, Piper was atop the helpless, hopping prey.

Growls overtook peeps. Then, in one striking snap, silence.

A community of birds screeched, the usual early-morning chirps of birdsong replaced by quick piercing cries of nesting baby birds, distressed by the predatory scene below. A long shriek followed each avian SOS, the dual notes of adult birds sending out alarms. The sight and sounds drove my hands deep into my ribs, just above my empty womb.

On the ground the bird lay lifeless. It had not been able to fly above and away from its predator. What should have played out as an amusing scene – dog pawing upward, dancing on hind legs, a tiny bird safe in flight – turned into a natural catastrophe.

The screech-filled sky grew louder as the dog examined its victim, sniffing the stench of blood, rolling the feathered carcass with a paw. Oak leaves swished like protesting placards against the sky. The bird could not fly, I kept thinking, even before the attack.

In his scissors bite, Piper carried his prize to me and placed it, as if a gift, at my feet. I fell to my knees. Tears streamed down my face, some dropping on the dog's evenly clipped white muzzle. Twisting his snout, right to left, right to left, his eyes swept mine as if confused. Where was the pat, the treat, the praise for this flawless execution of hunter instinct?

"Good dog," I said, still sobbing. I placed my hand on his stretched neck. I stroked down to his back and lifted my hand up again to his neck, over and over in a circular motion, acknowledging not his act of brutality, but its message. Had the dear, yet flawed, fetus I carried a month earlier, survived its passage from womb to world, the baby, like the bird, would still not have been able to fly.

"Let's go inside," I told the dog, He trotted obediently in front of me.

NOURISHING

A fter my miscarriage in 1985, I figured I'd play my cards extra carefully throughout my second pregnancy. I exercised, attended Lamaze classes, and even massaged my nipples - a suggestion right out of the *Le Leche League* pamphlets in the obstetrician's office. That way, my reasoning went, I could look forward to the ease of natural childbirth, immediately followed by the joyful bond of breastfeeding my newborn.

No deal. On either count.

I threw in my lousy hand on the baby-by-birth-canal ante after over a full day of labor. Twenty-five years later, I still can't look at an orange Popsicle without retching. After all that contracting and gagging - the doctor decided I should go C-section. Erratic peaks and troughs on the fetal monitor indicated the unborn baby was experiencing increased trauma. In less than a half hour a surgeon slit my lower abdomen and lifted the baby out.

Sustaining Baby Emily by mother's milk, however, was the losing hand I refused to let go of.

It's no wonder that during first attempts in the hospital, my breast and my baby didn't "latch on," the actual term for a successful nursing connection. Under the pharmaceutical influence of Tylox, a narcotic analgesic prescribed to ease post-surgery pain, I wasn't playing this breastfeeding game with a full deck, so to speak. There is a photograph of me, two hours post-Caesarean, surrounded by Larry and my relieved parents and in-laws.

They appear to be smiling above a cadaver.

I felt no pain, but I didn't feel much of anything else either. Except itchy. Very, very itchy. Even under the best of circumstances, my first attempts to breastfeed Baby Emily might have been challenging. Mother deer guide their newborn fawns to their nourishing nipples in the pitch of primeval darkness. They have their babies up on all fours a half-hour after birth too. Humans lack these smarts.

Which is fine, I believe in education - public even. If I thought I needed to be formally taught, step-by-step, the *natural* art of breastfeeding, you could have assigned me a seat, front- row, center. I would have hung on to every word of instruction, taken notes, and asked questions. Instead, a nurse just plopped the infant in my arms - arms that would be taking signals from my drugged head. Then she scooted out the door to her next patient. When she returned and observed my failed attempt, she took Emily and lowered her back into the infant cart beside me. "*We'll* try again later," she said, wheeling the baby out the door. At least that's how I remember it through my post-natal buzz.

From what I had read, I was aware that babies born to sedated mothers often have poor sucking reflexes. That's why I opted a spinal block over anesthesia for the C-section. That way, the numbing effect would not be felt by the child in utero - or out. Still, she too had struggled through 26 hours of labor. This underscores why, along with the maternal reflex that "lets down" breast milk not kicking in, the baby's sucking reflex wasn't up to par. We were both the birthing wounded trying to win the Battle of the Breast.

Or maybe I should say boob. That's how I felt anyway - like a boob. My inability to achieve a let-down, another breastfeeding term, was keeping breast milk – the best possible nourishment – from my baby. I remembered reading that formula didn't provide the real thing's resistance to infection and food allergies either. I was letting the baby down instead of letting the milk down.

Still, through all the soft sucking there was ne'er a trickle. Milk, nevertheless, was collecting in the mammary glands. My breasts grew rock hard. . . . mountainous. But there was not a drop to drink.

Early into the baby's two-day stay in pediatric intensive care (for observation after her stressful labor) I was handed a manual breast pump to "express" myself, another piece of *La Leche League* lingo. Picture placing the flared bell of a bicycle horn over an aching, swollen breast. Now honk the horn's rubber bulb. Keep honking, again and again. Fifteen, twenty minutes.

An ounce of mother's milk at last filled the glass I held just below my sore nipple. This was a mixed blessing, for the baby drank it through the rubbery nipple of the nursing bottle. The practice – through her short stay in ICU – could further impede her motivation to take the breast.

And then, through a few more days of questionable infant weight gain, milking my breasts by hand – it worked better than the bicycle horn – and breast-milk-by-bottle, one of us (or maybe both) got the hang of it. Her two tiny lips suddenly latched onto my nipple like prickly on a pup's paw. Baby Emily's mouth almost entirely surrounded the areola as she sucked madly, milk spilling out of the corners of her mouth.

I felt an unquestionable tug, a sustained tingle coming from the full flow of this milky pipeline. The sensation, almost sexual: mother and child soaked, satisfied. One of us crying over a bum deal played out to a royal flush.

Kɪᴅ Lɪᴛ

Once upon a time a little boy who loved a family of ducklings married a little girl who adored a family of bears. . .

"This one," Conor insists. He digs out a worn, hardcover book and presses it into his father's thigh. "Do this one."

I can still see my son in his baggy dinosaur pjs, begging Larry to put aside the storybooks we had carried home from the library that day and give in to his pleas to read *Make Way for Ducklings*. The dog-eared copy had actually belonged to Larry when he was Conor's age.

It wasn't the first time young Conor chose this book. Just as Larry used to beg his mother to read the half-century old classic about a family of mallards that settles in Boston, so would Conor invoke the book's characters, all seriousness in his footed sleepwear, one night after the other.

"The ducks 'n Offsir Mike."

Officer Michael fascinated our son. Conor leaned closer to the page whenever Larry got to the part about how the man-in-blue would plant himself in the center of a city street, raise his white-gloved hand to stop busy Boston traffic, and then direct seven ducklings safely across the road. Jack, Kack, Lack, Mack, Nack, Ouack, and Pack followed. The magical scene now mesmerized a second generation of Haydens.

When Larry was in third grade, he and his family moved to Enfield from nearby Springfield, Massachusetts. The town had doubled its population in ten years with its proliferation of ranches, capes, and split-levels that replaced former farms. The familiar landscape of Larry's urban childhood – city sidewalks, traffic lights, and store-fronts reminiscent of the illustrations of Boston in *Make Way for Ducklings* – had vanished in suburbia.

One afternoon, unbeknownst to his parents, nine-year-old Larry introduced himself to his new Connecticut neighbors as *Michael*, as in Officer Michael. His use of an alias was not discovered until early evening, when a neighbor called Larry's mother to ask if *Michael* could stay for dinner.

"Michael who?" my future mother-in-law replied.

Michael who? Indeed. Safe-keeper of endangered species.

My favorite children's story was *Blueberries for Sal*, a picture book about a family of bears. Little more than a sidewalk maple and back-yard fig tree grew in the Brooklyn neighborhood of my youth. But my family did spend one week every summer in an upstate New York cabin on the edge of the Catskill Mountains. The bungalow housed a potbel-lied stove, just like the one in the picture of Sal's mother's kitchen on the book's inside cover. The dotted curtains, framed clock, and three-pronged towel racks in the tiny cottage seemed pretty much the same too. I didn't own a copy of *Blueberries for Sal* – we were library goers – but I could remember every picture on every page.

Every year in the Catskills, my Mom, Dad, and twin brother – who is also named Larry – would hunt for huckleberries during our week away from the city. Whether I realized it or not, I carried a recollection of Sal's blueberry-picking adventure with me and my tiny tin pail, on ev-ery huckleberry hunt. What if, I wondered, like the child in *Blueberries for Sal*, I wandered away from my Mom, trading places with an errant baby bear so that – like Little Bear and Little Sal's mother, and Little Sal and Little Bear's mother – we got all mixed up with each other among the berry bushes on the upstate New York hill?

I moved to Enfield when I was ten, a year or so after my future husband's family settled there. We lived, maybe, two miles apart. But it wasn't only geography that brought us together fifteen years later. Like any couple meant to live and love one another, our pasts somehow synchronized with our presents.

In time the little boy who loved a family of ducklings married the little girl who adored the family of bears. We had, after all, faced our opposing forces and experienced the transformational magic of love. Then, one Christmas before we had children, Larry's mother, the wise Fairy Parent, I guess, presented Larry and I with gifts - brand new copies of the books we had always called our favorite childhood tales. It was then we discovered what she already knew. Both of our favorite books, however different in their city and country settings, were penned by the same author - Robert McCloskey.

Coincidence? About as much, I say, as the star pattern in a cross-cut apple or the flower outline on the underside of a sand dollar. In matters of the heart there is little need for proof - just connection. Like the way McCloskey's words and pictures connected Larry and I to his characters - and possibly, each other.

In time Larry and I had three wishes granted: each other, our daughter, and our son. By then our McCloskey books had become more than just favorite stories. They offered new ways of seeing the world: raising our own brood of ducklings, our own pack of cubs. Eventually, reading to our children gave us the chance to reacquaint ourselves – page by page – with the powerful images. We reread our favorites through fresh eyes. Larry would point to the pictures in *Make Way for Ducklings* that transfixed him as a kid, now with his own son on his knee.

"Look how much the ducks look like real ducks - and the people look like cartoons," he'd say, his fingers directing Conor's stare.

I'd put down *Blueberries for Sal* after reading it to my daughter Emily, realizing how the sounds of its words delighted my ear as much as its resolution pleased my heart. *Kuplink, kuplank, kuplunk.* I can still hear Sal's berries hit the bottom of the pail. There was music, too, in the way the mix of mother, child, bear, and cub played. I never feared each creature would not find its proper place in the hillside symphony.

A family of ducks on a city street. A family of bears in the wild. Little did Larry and I, as youngsters, know that our favorite childhood stories would, in time, connect us to one another and guide us through our own domains - domestic and wild.

Once upon a time.

Our Fathers

I

My long-time pastor, Father Francis Kerwan, had it in mind for me to commit three years of Sundays to the distribution of Holy Communion among the parishioners of Holy Family Church. Both families – Larry's and mine – worshiped there since he founded the parish in the mid-1960s. While the new church was still in construction, we attended Mass in the auditorium of the high school where I was a freshman. When we looked up, we'd see pens and pencils jutting out of the high ceiling, projectiles antsy students had thrown, like darts at a corkboard, during school assemblies and study halls held in the vast room.

The auditorium became our weekly sanctuary for about a year. Row after row of padded seats faced the makeshift altar onstage. Whenever Father, while celebrating Mass, came to a part that required kneeling – which was impossible – he would look to his parishioners and say, "Assume a prayerful position." My mother loved to tell that story to her sisters and brother in New York.

Larry and I married at Holy Family. We christened our daughter and son there. Now the two of us sat every week, with our toddler and baby, in the sound-proof children's room in the rear of the church. When I attended alone, I chose a back pew.

Why would Father Kerwan ask me to become a Eucharistic Minister? I could think of much more worthy people to serve communion on the altar and deliver it to homebound parishioners. How could I, the more likely of my children's parents to get cranky, swear, or hold a grudge, make the short list for what Father called "a special ministry?"

In my mind, Larry was the better candidate. He had started the un-employment support group that met in the church hall every Sunday night. He helped chop down and put up the Holy Family Christmas tree each winter, and brought out the booths for the church fair each summer. He wasn't the one who once made a remark to Father – a remark that some might consider impertinent.

The remark slipped out when Larry and I sat with Father, six months before our wedding, to make the date official. Records had to be documented; applications had to be filled out. When Father asked for my address, after recording Larry's on a marriage registra-tion form, I paused. Larry and I lived together. That didn't shake up too many people in the Seventies, but – Father wasn't *many people* – Father was a *man of God*.

"Same address as Larry," I said slightly hesitant.

"I see," Father said. I don't think he was shocked. He looked more, I'd say, circumspect. He had the authority to say we couldn't get married in the church.

Father knew, all too well, that – up to just recently – Larry and I were forced to put off our marriage precisely because we wanted to get married in a Catholic church. Larry was divorced. Father had advised him through an annulment, a process that can revoke a mar-riage in the eyes of the church the way divorce voids a union in the eyes of the law. This had taken over three years - the same three years we had been together. During the last year, Larry and I had "cohabitated," according to the legal language of church and state.

"We don't feel we should have to lie about it," said Larry. He spoke to a man who understood how grueling an annulment tribunal – the official court of the church – could be. There are countless forms and interrogations about personal, psychologi-cal, and even intimate behaviors directed to the former husband and wife. Family members are asked to verify or witness the written testimonies. Larry's former spouse could have contested. She didn't. Even so, the upheaval Larry went through before the official dissolution of vows took an emotional toll. Father had no hand in the deanery proceedings. An annulment is subject to district, not parish, rule.

Larry had a previous dealing with the official district as a member of Holy Family Church, years before the annulment - when he led the very first Holy Family basketball team to the Deanery Championship in 1967. I wonder if Father remembered that championship game as he shook his head at my "Same as Larry" reply to his question about my home address. His head of hair was full and black back then, and he wore silver metal eyeglass frames with black plastic brow lines. Father had been so proud of the young players. Clapped and cheered so hard at the deciding game, his glasses fell through the bleachers. Father peered through thicker lenses now. Wider frames. Horn-rimmed.

Larry and I could have been married by a justice of the peace or in an Episcopalian church without having to wait. Why were we putting ourselves through the delay, the awkwardness?

The annulment meant more to our parents. Both families had close ties with the spirit and structure of Holy Family Church, a modern, well run house of worship. Larry's Dad was a Sunday usher. My mother cooked for Father Kerwan when the rectory housekeeper was away.

There was also the letter Larry's dad wrote to him, his oldest child, three years earlier, just before he underwent open heart surgery. "Take care of your mother if anything happens. And from the bottom of my heart I ask you to follow through with the annulment." His father got through the operation. Larry survived the church version of divorce court.

Father went on with our prenuptial meeting and my unsatisfactory answer to his question. "The church asks that your engagement be a time of grace and growth in preparing for your marriage. . ." he began.

And that's when impertinent me butted in with, "But Father." He looked surprised that I had started to speak in the middle of his sincere, yet succinct talk about starting our relationship anew now that we were engaged, reconciling with God, separating until the wedding day.

"Excuse me father," I tried to soften my interruption. "I feel as if that's exactly what we have achieved by living together."

Father didn't speak. His eyes behind his dark-framed glasses widened. I went on.

"We've both grown spiritually, Father. Larry's going back to church, I'm teaching religious instructions and . . ."

Now Father stopped me in mid-sentence. "I recognize that, Laura. But the church believes living chastely during your remaining months of engagement will teach you many things about one another."

"But we're thirty years old," said Larry. I didn't know what else to say.

There was an awkward silence. Then Father began writing, until he laid the pen down to say, "Then I ask you to pray upon it."

"That we can do Father," I said.

"Yes, Father," Larry agreed.

"As will I," said this Man of God who reached over to shake Larry's hand. "Now you must sign these," he said, passing the registration papers over the desk. As I wrote my name on the marriage registry I saw that Father had written my parents' address next to my name. He opened a large, leather-bound book. "Now let's see what dates are available in August, shall we?"

Six months after we were married, Father had us running the parish engaged couples program. Now he wanted me to be a Eucharistic Minister.

I graduated from a Catholic college, the greater percentage of its faculty made up of some mighty savvy Sisters of Mercy. Ones who wrote Christmas plays – in Latin – performed experiments on moon rocks, and even, it was rumored, offered their own Masses on campus, a direct violation of church law that allowed only male celebrants.

The prospect of church reform filled the air as much as political reform did in those days of Vietnam War protests and Women's Rights marches. Pope John Paul XXIII's Vatican II proclamations had opened the church door –a crack – by changing the traditional Latin Mass to English and turning the altar so that the priest faced his parishioners during services. These nuns who taught most of my college classes – some of whom wore everyday clothes instead of habits – showed me, semester after semester, that the Catholic patriarchy needed to reach out and offer a firmer handshake to the women of the church.

Recently, Holy Family Church had started referring to altar boys as altar servers and invited a few young girls into the religious rank. Could altar girls and female Eucharistic Ministers in the Nineties lead to women priests in the twenty-first century, I thought? I have to admit; my saying yes to Father Kerwan's offer to become a Eucharistic Minister may have had more to do with religious politics than goodness and personal growth.

Even if these reasons to heed his call had not begun to surface, I could no more say no to Father Kerwan than the disciples could have refused their calling. He and I spoke regularly on the phone, lining up engaged couples meetings. We would talk business as well as chat about his golf swing and those *God-love-them Red Sox*. Father had a habit – intentional or not, I'm not sure – of not identifying himself on the phone. His strong Irish voice was all the introduction he needed.

One day the phone rang.

"Laura, I want you to be a Eucharistic minister."

"This is either Father Kerwan – or the voice of God – and I can't say no to either," I replied. Besides, I owed him one.

II

Around the time late summer's leaves changed their color, dried, and began to fall, my Eucharistic minister orientation was underway. I would start official duty in December. There was necessary protocol to practice: carrying the ciborium (which held the hosts), placing an unblessed host in the mouth or hand of the communicant, storing the unused wafers.

What a relief, through this training ritual, to hear Father Kerwan say that, as sacred and solemn as the distribution of the Eucharistic was, we new recruits – there were three of us – should not take ourselves too seriously.

"Every tongue upon which you lay the host will be different," he said, as only a poker-faced Irish pastor could. Still, the eyes behind his glasses twinkled as he spoke, just as at my high school graduation, wedding, and Emily and Conor's baptisms.

Well into my training, Father Kerwan had come across my father's name on a list of outpatients during one of his regular visits to hospitalized parishioners. Dad was getting radiation treatments for lung cancer. Soon afterward, Father appeared at my parents' front door on an afternoon when the children and I were visiting.

Father had always gotten a charge out of the transplanted New Yorkers in the parish. The ones who, like my Dad, wound up working at an engineering plant in the middle of Connecticut tobacco fields, after the company closed its business offices on Madison Avenue. They joked together, drank together, played golf together.

Father walked into my parents' home as a neighbor might, a neighbor with important business. He bent to give Mom a hug, and then went over to Dad, who was sitting at the dining room table in his pajamas and robe, doing a crossword puzzle. His hand touched Dad's shoulder.

"What's this I hear at the hospital, Jim?"

Father Kerwan could broach matters of mortality as smoothly as he could sink a birdie putt – his aim exacting and calm. And so, as if teeing up from one hole to the next, he and Dad addressed the bloody cough, the shadowy x-ray, the diagnosis of lung cancer, and the long shot to shrink the tumor.

Father knew it wasn't lack of faith that kept my father away from Sunday Mass once his treatment began. Dad had cut himself off from his public exercise of faith – in pew eight, just right of the center aisle – because he did not want to have to explain why his hair seemed to vanish from one week to the next, or to reveal his steady but labored breathing to his friends in the parish. Father blessed my parents and their home before he left.

III

As a ten-year-old, I didn't know too much, but I knew my parents were always right. That is not to say they did not make mistakes, but in my mind, there was no question about the correctness of their errors.

Mom, Dad, my twin brother Larry and I had just spent a week away from Brooklyn. It was our yearly retreat to a country bunga-low complete with pot-bellied stove and paperbacks. Mom always seemed to get halfway through the same book.

For my brother and I there was great fun in those purple Catskill hills. We tubed down a river that actually popped with fish, swam in a crystal lake, and bicycled on a gravel hill so steep we had to steer in long, side-to-side S's to get to the top. Wurtsboro was just about as far from Brooklyn as the sun is from the moon.

During our stay Mom and Dad smiled a lot and turned browner than at any other time of the year. Once on the screened porch, I heard Mom whisper, "Wouldn't it be nice?" They were different there. Dad spent the whole day in baggy pants and a white T-shirt. He fished for catfish and Mom cleaned and fried the catch for din-ner.

Once we went fishing off a lakeside landing. There were people on every side of us. Someone pulled his rod back and forth and got his fishhook stuck in Dad's arm. It bled so much I was afraid he was going to die. I cried, but Dad just clipped off one end of that hook and slid it like an unthreaded needle stitched through his skin.

We left our summer get-away on a Saturday afternoon, after Mom finished washing the kitchen floor. As we approached our street, most of our Brooklyn neighbors sat on the steamy stoops of their brick, four-family homes. Noisy players socked pink rubber balls on the sidewalk. Squatting between cars, two boys started to scream, " Car, car, C-A-R, stick your head in T-A-R," to drivers passing by. Their oft-repeated chant stopped at "stick" when they recognized our Plymouth.

The next Monday morning, Dad left for work in a suit and tie. On his walk to the train, he was greeted by a pigeon above him and then a wet splat on the side of his head. He came right back home, where he slipped into the bathroom with Mom and quickly emerged with a slick head of water-smacked hair. "Good luck!" he muttered abruptly as he shot out the front door. It almost sounded like a question.

Six o'clock that evening the neighborhood trembled as the "L" rumbled in and out of the New Utretch Avenue Station. By 6:10 Dad walked through the door of our apartment, his expression much too severe to still be fixed on the morning's dirty bird. His tie turned crooked under his collar. The shirt puffed sloppily above his belt. If I didn't know better, I'd have guessed that sticks filled his pant legs and lead, his shoes.

He looked more himself by dinnertime, but he had some news that was as unexpected as his earlier appearance. "The company's moving to Connecticut," was all I let myself hear. Mom seemed to lose the color in her face as she listened to the details. I cried as my thoughts shouted my own questions. *Where was this place anyway? Who lived there? Did its beaches have parachute rides?*

We took three road trips to this northern state. Between pouts I kept busy with the usual spotting of out-of-state license plates and counting of telephone poles. I played even more serious games in my head. *What if I lived here? Who goes to this school anyway?* Even though Connecticut looked so different – tobacco farms, shingled, single-family homes, no sidewalk or stoops – it had a Carvel ice cream store, just like Brooklyn.

On the third visit Dad and Mom bought a home, picked out a lot, and asked for two extra outlets on the breezeway. My usual move in a game I couldn't win was to quit. I couldn't exactly quit my family. It was easier to pout and cry.

The eve of the move remains a blur of aunts, uncles, cousins, and neighbors hugging, kissing, and patting me. I felt like an abused puppy. When everyone finally left, the four of us paced through the rooms full of boxes that use to be our home. Mom's face was worn when she said, "Best get to bed. Tomorrow's a big day."

Lying wide awake, I focused on each corner of the room. The walls were as bare as the ceilings. I thought I could weep myself to a soft sleep that would dream away tomorrow's move. The tears came, but not the peace.

I slipped out of bed and walked toward Mom and Dad's room. Their bedroom light assured me they were still awake as it provided a safe path through the cluttered hallway. Then something made me stop at their door. Dad's back was turned to me and Mom grasped his shoulder . . . no . . . her arms wrapped around him. His head rested on *her* shoulder. He shook. And he sobbed, "I don't know Dee, I just don't know."

The next day I held my pet turtles in a dish in the back seat of the 1955 Plymouth. I braced the bowl against my knees to keep my hard-shelled pets from shaking. Silent, but dry-eyed, I sat through the three-hour ride to Connecticut, steadying my turtles all the way.

IV

I drove my parents home from the UConn Medical Center through a heavy late afternoon rain on Halloween night, 1988. The doctor had not ended this visit with one of her usual "cancer isn't the scary word it was twenty years ago," epigrams. Nor had she reminded us how healthfully her own father had survived lung cancer. How could she, after breaking the news that Dad's tumor was not operable, that chemotherapy would be added to the radiation treatment, and that eventually all that could be done for the patient would be to keep him as comfortable as possible?

I could not think about the final touches I had planned to make on Emily and Conor's Minnie Mouse and dinosaur Halloween costumes. Larry would have to take care of those and bring them to the town party. I would remain with Mom and Dad.

At church the next morning – the Feast of All Saints – Father Kerwan stopped me after Mass.

"How's Jim?" he asked,

I could not find the words to tell him that, in the time it takes a newborn to poke and creep, my father would fade and vanish. I just said, "He's a real trooper. He's doing the best he can." And then I had a bold thought, but I offered it to Father anyway. "Can I bring Dad communion?" I wouldn't be an official Eucharistic minister for a few weeks. The newly trained recruits usually began distributing communion just before Christmas, to get them ready for the holiday rush to services.

"I can think of no better start," said Father as he put his hand on my shoulder.

I entered the sanctuary alone, found the carrying pouch for the host and the key to the tabernacle. This was a sacred territory I had not yet officially crossed.

Within minutes after leaving the church I began the ritual of home communion at my parents' dining room table. We blessed ourselves

> *In the name of the Father, and of the Son, and of the Holy Spirit.*

I held the host between his face and mine. My hands shook.

> *This is the Lamb of God who takes away the sins of the world. Happy are those who are called to his supper.*

Dad, whose body appeared to have aged two decades in two months, knew well the layman's reply. With great reverence he said,

> *Lord I am not worthy to receive you but only say the word and I shall be healed.*

I paused. Almost stopped altogether. I wanted to say, "But Dad, no man is worthier," for I knew no man hungered more for this spiritual food than he. Instead, I kept with the sacred script, holding the Host before him in our presence.

> *The Body of Christ.*

V

A late March snow covered the oak leaves on Dad's front lawn the morning of his death. I remembered that the first discomfort of his disease was that he could not rake them away last fall.

I found a prayer card to the patron saint of work on his dresser the morning we returned from the hospital without him. Worn at the edges from frequent handling, it began

> *Oh Saint Joseph, who blended skill with charity, we praise you! With you, silent carpenter, as our guide, help us to do the work you have asked and come to the rewards you have promised.*

My father faced his last days and his God with the humility he revealed every day. If an unpretentious soul can "Ah shucks" it in the afterlife, my father has found his everlasting niche. Yet, even the strongest spiritual assurances cannot entirely replace, for me, the father who escorted a daughter down a church aisle, a grandfather who played peek-a-boo on his hands and knees, a master homemade pasta maker and tomato harvester.

As a staid parent, I explain to my children that Grandpa is in heaven now. Yet, the forty-year-old child in me can do little to hold back tears when, I go to his closet and hear my five-year-old daughter say, "Grandpa doesn't need his clothes in heaven." My son, who just turned three, still tells me not to sit in Grandpa's chair.

Somehow in death, though, Dad grew larger than life. His obituary headline read, "World War II Code-breaker" even though he never admitted to being more than a telegraph operator. Friends from work shared stories of his compassion. How he would let a new father on the staff take a quick nap in his office. Like the poet Wordsworth's response to a rainbow, my heart leaps at the sound of these stories about my father.

I take his daily prayer to Saint Joseph the Worker and use his tomato cages in my garden this year.

THE WRITING ON THE CEILING

The first lesson of the Cub Scout campout at Westover Air Force Base appeared scrawled across the crossbeam of a dingy hooch. The message, left by an unidentified Air Force camper, read: *So This Isn't Home-Deal with It.* The den leader pointed it out in response to a cacophony of complaints targeted at the accommodations his boys were about to settle into for the weekend.

"It's a hooch, not a hotel," he said matter-of-factly. *Very far from a hotel*, I thought as Conor and I helped assemble thirty-three cots across the floor and hang a sky-blue plastic tarp on the far end of the stark structure. The plastic would divide two other mothers and me from fifteen eight-year-old boys and their dads.

It seemed hours had passed since our caravan of cars pulled into the Base parking lot in teeming October rain. A clear, beaded curtain of drops cascaded between the outdoors and the open-ended rear of the Air Force truck that transported us from parking lot to campsite. Now, almost lunchtime, those rain beads steadily pelted the roof of our hooch with no sign of letup.

For the time being at least, Conor and I remained dry inside the crude wood-planked shelter. I tried not to think about the Frankies' Firehouse pizza my husband Larry and daughter Emily would be sitting down to in the next hour, as they celebrated the end of the soccer season for the U-12 Pink Panthers,

Father and daughter, mother and son. Not the usual combinations. Yet that was only the start of the turnabouts that would occur on this weekend that was supposed to bring my son a little closer to the threshold of manhood. Since Larry coached Emily's soccer team, it made more sense for me to accompany Conor on the Air

Force Base overnighter. The Pink Panthers had games scheduled for both Saturday and Sunday.

When she entered sixth grade a month earlier, Emily had already begun to experience lesson after lesson about "dealing with" not-so-ideal conditions. She had been carrying more than her usual load of school, soccer, and piano lessons. Taking on the co-director duties of the annual Hazardville Memorial Talent Show wasn't quite what made the difference, either.

The additional weight had come out of the blue, in the local news of a tragic car accident.

Emily did not actually know the middle-school boy who had been killed by a van while riding his bike around a nasty curve on South Maple Road. Her friends, including her fellow Talent Show directors, did. Although he was older than these girls, he had gone to Hazardville Memorial, so some of her friends reacted to the awful news more personally than she. During one after-school rehearsal, Michelle broke down in tears recalling how the boy used to say hi to her in the hallway last year. Shannon lost her composure over the thought of the accident victim having shared middle-school labs with her older sister. Tina simply freaked after Julie figured out that she happened to sit in the same sixth-grade seat, in the classroom the boy occupied a year ago.

Emily, however, had no direct tie, which explains, perhaps, how through this early experience with death, she was able to offer the strong shoulder for her friends to cry on. After each rehearsal that week before the end of soccer season, I watched her hug one friend after the other, making several rounds among the sixth-graders before leaving school. She was quieter than usual at home those evenings.

I had talked to Emily about the accident after reading about it, but the focus had not been the victim, whom we really didn't know. Truth is, if the unidentified graffiti artist up at Westover had access to the ceiling of our home, *Nothing's Simple - Deal with It,* would have been an appropriate adage for the facts of sixth-grade life and death I had begun to share with my daughter.

Fact number one – tragedies happen to innocent people. The boy had done nothing wrong.

Fact number two – good people can do bad things. Emily's Brownie troop leader, the mother of one of her classmates, had driven the fatal van.

How does an eleven-year-old even start to wrap her mind around the notion that the woman, who had taught her the "Brownie Smile Song" and never forgot the graham crackers, marshmallows, and chocolate bars for S'mores around the campfire, was also the person responsible for the boy's death? Her troop leader had been driving the same big old blue Chevy van in which she had given the two of us a number of rides, up and down winding Berkshire hills, to overnight Brownie campouts. That same blue van just didn't maneuver correctly around that South Maple Street curve, not even an eighth of a mile from its home driveway. When it swerved to the right, it hit the boy.

As the news spread, I watched for Emily's response as I looped through the complications myself, like a passenger on a Six Flags rollercoaster. Within the extremes of easy or difficult, love or hate, right or wrong, I watched to see if she, like me, was turning over and over through the tracks of the local main attractions: an innocent life lost, grieving friends, affection for her former leader, and empathy for her daughter. I wondered how she could continue to be, as her Brownie troop leader had taught her, a friend to all and a sister to every other Scout.

Yet she seemed fine as she got ready for her last soccer weekend of the season and Conor and I headed up to the Westover campsite in the steady, heavy rain. The Cub Scout overnight was touted as a weekend when boys would start to become men on military terrain. While official vehicles trucked in load after load of duffel- bag- hauling youngsters and their Dads, the early arrivals began to spread the word that there were empty bullet shells scattered over the rain-drenched landscape. Young Scouts began combing the terrain as if mining for gold, returning with their pockets bulging. Conor collected fourteen spent shells, a measly stash compared to forty scavenged by his den leader's son.

The young troopers carried their bullet bounty to the mess hall hooch where Military Ready-to Eat lunches filled their y-chromosonal hungers. Each MRE pouch came with the same directions: smack onto a hard surface, wait four minutes (as it magically heated the food), open carefully, chow down. The meals were difficult to distinguish from one another, but we were pretty sure we had the makings of chicken chow "mush", "mangled" eggs, and pot "rust" at our table. Sundry extras, too: a Tom Thumb-size bottle of Tabasco sauce, Hershey bars, and matches. The cuisine, in an eight-year-old Cub's mind, could only be superseded by the next activity of the day: tip-to-tail tour of a war plane and, the *piece d' resistance* of the boys-to-men weekend, a firing range demonstration the next morning.

When Conor and I signed up for this weekend getaway, I had no idea that, after a sleepless overnight in a chilly hooch, even greater discomfort lay ahead. Yet, when I think back to how excitedly these boys collected empty rifle shells the soggy morning before, I can begin to understand their fervor at the prospect of being placed behind an M16, the same firearm turned household word by Hollywood's man of men, Rambo himself, Sylvester Stallone.

The two other mothers who marched along with me through this military camp were totally turned on by the prospect of squeezing the triggers of these metal-fuckers. The man in charge led them over to an even more powerful M60, Stallone's wipeout weapon at the end of his classic 2007 flick. Next thing I knew, the two had dubbed themselves *Rambo Moms* as each one dug her heels into the ground, raised the heavy weapon to her shoulder and aimed. The female forms shook through long, loud rat-a-tat-tats. Fired up, they shot over and over, with that, "I wanna kill, kill, KILL" look Arlo Guthrie gets when he sings "Alice's Restaurant" onstage. His face gets tight. His eyes squint. He starts bouncing up and down in his seat, but – and this is a big but – Arlo's's faking the killer instinct to appear psycho in his performance. The guy in his anti-war anthem of the Sixties wants to appear so crazed that an Army recruiter says, "Sorry, we want soldiers, but we can't trust you with that weapon," and defers him. These ladies came across as serious as streaming bullets.

I watched for a while, careful not to say too much. Then one after the other – Den Leader, Scout Master, and Military Reservist – egged me on to pick up an M16.

"It's philosophy, not fear," I shot back as if words were my ammunition. That disarmed their insistence, though not their disbelief. They could no more relate to me not wanting to gun down a wooden target than they could share my one reservation about the Boy Scouts of America – that they are supported by the NRA.

I didn't engage in much conversation with the big boys or girls as we walked off the range. Conor never seemed to mind that his Mom didn't take the military stand and run a line of ammo through the magazine of an M16. Like everything else that weekend – the rain, a crude and chilly shelter – he took each make-em-a-man rung on the Boy Scouting ladder the way he used to tackle playground attractions in his nursery-school days, ricocheting from swing to slide to teeter-totter without missing a beat. He left no more or less infatuated with guns than he had been a week ago.

I didn't expect the final hours of the weekend to merge the separate activities of father and daughter, mother and son. It was sort of like the way pretend-assassin Arlo spends so much time, after introducing Alice and her restaurant in the very beginning of his convoluted ballad, to get back to her in the end. His roundabout storytelling escorts us through a Stockbridge churchyard and garbage dump, onto a local jail and, of course, an Army recruitment center, before Alice reappears in the last measures of the twenty minute tune.

By the time Larry, Emily, Conor and I had collectively gone through our separate yet simultaneous Frankie's pizza, MREs, trophy presentations, and firearms fest, we were finally back to being a foursome, wrapping the weekend up before the start of the school and work week. After dinner Conor showed Larry his shell collection and demonstrated how he stood behind an M16, shaking his body like the bowl of a Sunbeam mixmaster. It was around then that I noticed my usually even-tempered daughter acting pretty edgy, curt, almost sullen.

"What's wrong?" I ask once, twice, three times through the early evening.

"Nothing," she said a few times. This evolved to a more honest, "I don't know," followed by a damn good cry in which – and here's where Alice is about to enter the song again – Emily's body shook and rattled just as convulsively as her brother Conor's had, reverberating to the trail of bullets he triggered through the M16 earlier that day. My son, who had glimpsed the threshold of adulthood that weekend, had not changed nearly as much as his stay-at-home sis, caught in the backlash of her close friends' grief. Strong Emily, supportive Emily, consoling Emily had come to realize that life does not last forever. And she had to deal with it.

BACKLASH

Larry had tacked a funny newspaper clipping, "A Dad's 10 Rules for Dating His Daughter," onto the kitchen bulletin board just before his hospitalization. I turned to the guidelines, still posted, a month after he died. It suggested dating venues with police or nuns in sight.

Without even realizing it, Emily complied. "This is Michael." She introduced the blonde boy after a teen get-together at church. I knew his family from school and sporting events. His dad coached Saturday afternoon basketball as Larry had. The red-faced lad nodded and I smiled back.

We're going out," she gushed in the car on the way home – eighth- grade lingo for when the couple sits together in the lunchroom, phones once or twice after school (this was before cell phones would connect teens 24/7), and hangs out as a twosome at Galactic Bowling.

Under usual circumstances I would have considered this a wholesome rite of passage, but I worried that her ear-to-ear grin indicated she was *too happy* for a child who had just lost her father. Maybe she just seemed over-the-top elated because I was below-the-bottom sad. I called our pediatrician.

"Gerry, I know this sounds weird, but it's like Emily has stopped grieving."

"I wouldn't be *too* concerned." he said. "If I didn't know her since the day she was born, I might say otherwise."

The doctor had a deep concern for Emily and Conor. They were the kids of the guy he bred fruit flies with in 10th grade biology class. Larry never threw out the doctor's impromptu sketch of him from their college days. The cartoon – scrawled on lined notebook paper – depicted Larry's jutting chin (with stubble) along with his long and bushy sideburns – chops he called them. No, it wasn't just the local doctor who went on to say, "Emily's always been a resilient child." It was the friend who asked Larry to be best man at his wedding, shortly after she was born.

Was resilient just a nice word for strong-willed? Stubborn, even? I wondered. If so, the acorn hadn't fallen far from Mother Oak. Whenever I would dig my heels into one side of an argument, I had a hard time letting up. Larry often reminded me that the small stuff – what who said to whom, or worse, what who *implied* to whom – didn't matter in the big picture, a picture he saw more clearly than I.

Was Emily forcing herself not to grieve? Hiding her turmoil by going through the motions of control?

I remembered how she had fussed whenever I breast-fed her baby brother. Not yet two years old, Em would lose interest in her chunky Little People Fun Farm Friends – her big-sister gift when Conor was born – and try to climb onto my lap. When that didn't get her close enough to satisfy her urge for equal attention, she'd slide down and run off to find Baby - her favorite doll – the one that traveled to college with her sixteen years later, as love-worn as the *Velveteen Rabbit.* I was still feeding Conor when she returned, holding Baby horizontal across her chest. Her eyebrows furrowed above an intense stare shot at her infant brother's link to me. Eyes still fixed, she marched back and forth in front of us in almost military fashion, Baby firmly held across her heart.

"You think she's trying to get back at me for breastfeeding?" I asked Larry at dinner. "Show me if she can't be as close to me, she'll find that closeness somewhere else?"

He just shook his head. "Like mother, like daughter."

"What do you mean?" I wasn't sure if he was addressing the situation – mother feeding child – or mutual stubbornness.

"You decide." He winked. After dinner he turned his full attention to Em and her Fun Farm Friends while I fed our son.

Perhaps mothers do read too deeply into their daughter's behaviors. Try too hard to anticipate their needs and their motives. When Emily was ten she lost a tooth while at school. She was sent to the nurse to get a tiny case in which to carry it home safely. The thimble-sized container looked like a plastic treasure chest.

It wasn't until well after her mid-day return home that she said, "My tooth came out today. See?" She pulled up the rim of her mouth to show me the deep red empty space, in sharp contrast to her pink gum line.

"Well look at that," I said. "Where's the tooth?"

"Left it in my desk - in the box the nurse gave me." She sounded unfazed by it all. "The Tooth Fairy will find it."

I was not so unfazed. Though I kept calm on the outside, I panicked on the inside. Eight years old was too young for a mother-is-Tooth Fairy revelation. What would follow? Dad is Santa?

I needed a plan.

Emily had a piano lesson at 4:00 that afternoon. While she began playing scales with Mr. Patterson, I drove to her school, found her desk, took tooth, folded bill – over and over – and secured it in the plastic treasure chest. Made it back just as Em was on the last verse of *Camptown Races,* moving to a big *Oh, doo-dah-day!* finish.

When Emily got off the school bus the next day, I stood outside the door expecting to hear all about the tooth – and nothing but the tooth – from the end of the driveway. She didn't say a word. By the time she unpacked her lunch bag, we had still only engaged in everyday conversation. When she sat down to do her homework I finally blurted, "Well. Did the Tooth Fairy come?" much too excitedly.

"Oh yeah. The dollar's in my backpack," she said, unmoved.

Larry thought the escapade was a hoot – all that I-Love-Lucy style effort for so little return. Another sweetly ironic episode in the sitcom of our lives. I decided not to level with Emily, for fear of myth-busting the Tooth Fairy. I did wonder if she was onto my tooth game. Gettin' my goat. With a daughter it's hard to tell.

But Doctor Gerry had called her resilient as in able to roll with punches, even gut-wrenching ones. Resilient, I thought, as the daffodils that survived an April frost, the spring of her complicated birth. Resilient, as in the way she went right back to reading *A Tree Grows in Brooklyn* when she returned to school after her father's death.

She chose Betty Smith's classic because, like Francie Nolan, the novel's 14-year-old heroine, *I* grew up in Brooklyn too, the first granddaughter of immigrants. Francie pre-dated me by more than a generation, and she was Irish, not Italian, but the Nolan family's struggle to get by, like my grandparents' struggle, offered Em a glimpse of my family's hardscrabble past. In the 1930s my grandfather shined shoes in front of New York City banks. Grandma folded and twisted scraps of crepe paper into flowers at their flat in Hell's Kitchen. At night her daughters joined in the piecework to increase the family income.

A Tree Grows in Brooklyn seemed like a perfect choice for Emily. That is, until Chapter XXXVI, when Francie's father dies a week before Christmas, 1915. That was just about where Emily had read up to when Larry died, three weeks before Christmas, 1998.

"You don't have to finish the book," I told her. But she read onward, through Johnny Nolan's drunken demise to the end of the 400-page novel. Aced the assignment. I convinced myself she stuck with the book because she didn't really connect Johnny, a failed man, to the father she idolized, yet I worried that she still didn't seem to be reacting to her father's death.

A few months after Larry died I brought my children to see a child psychologist. Dr. Gerry agreed the visit would do no harm as we settled into our new, unsought normal. It would allow me to cover all bases in my attempt to mitigate their grief. Emily and Conor were hesitant, but said they would go along with the visit as long as I arranged for a family session instead of a one-on-one with a therapist.

We sat together. The doctor began by saying she was sorry for our loss. Then she directed a question to Emily.

"What happened?"

An uncomfortable silence followed. "Larry was recuperating," I began, but the look on the doctor's face, together with her second nod in Emily's direction quieted me. The doctor was well aware I could answer. The point was to get Emily to respond. But my daughter remained silent, avoided eye contact, and started to quietly cry. Whether the doctor liked it or not, I answered for Emily.

"Her father died when a blood clot in his leg traveled to his lung," I offered softly. This time the doctor let me trail through the details of the day I have relived, at first, every time I shut my eyes. Then, every time I was alone. And eventually, every time I would just zone out of the company I kept, recalling the minute by minute horror of the day Larry died.

"How do you know he died?" the doctor asked. Conor squirmed. Emily stared at her feet. "Did you see him?"

I added my own discomforted body language through her series of awkward questions: Who was in the casket? (Silence.) Was that really your father? (Confused expressions.) None of us understood that the doctor was trying to distinguish my children's memory of their father, in the funeral home, from their memories of him as an active and vital dad. Not until she said so.

With the exception of the *Who was in the casket?* line of inquiry, the children and I had already talked about her other focus that afternoon, the cause of Larry's death - the blot clot two weeks after surgery. She emphasized it was no one's fault. Just an unlucky tragedy. Like we didn't know that already.

That's how *I* remember the visit to the psychologist. Emily wrote about the appointment in her college application essay, four years later. This is most of her account.

> *I've been advised at various times in my life not to regret, but I can't help but feel bad about the attitude I carried with me to the psychologist. All I could think was how stupid an idea it was for me to discuss something so personal with a complete stranger. What did she know about me? My mom was insisting I see her because I didn't talk to her about what I was feeling since December, but I couldn't figure out what would inspire*

me to pour out my feelings to this doctor if I wouldn't do so with my own mother. So even though I knew my mom was older, wiser, and trying desperately to do what she could for her two mourning children, I still entered the psychologist's office with a bad attitude and a closed mind.

I don't really remember how the meeting started except that my brother, my mom, and I sat in a perfect semi-circle facing the psychologist. I have to admit I noticed the comfort of the chairs as informal small talk began. I politely responded. And I do remember the question: What happened? I remember my attitude, my resentment, and my lamentation. Most of all, I remember my refusal to talk. It seems like such a simple question, but let me assure you, it wasn't. At first I was confused. Why would she ask this? How could she not know what happened?

I answered the question in my head. "My dad died lady." I almost opened my mouth to say it. I could picture what her face would do. I'd gotten that "you poor baby" look countless times since December, and I didn't want to see it again. Besides, the word "died" sent chills through my body. I didn't want to say it. I didn't want to place it in the same sentence that would mention my dad. Saying it meant it really happened. I lived each day clinging to the hope that maybe it was a dream, and soon I would wake up to the sound of his voice warning me that I needed to get out of bed before I missed the school bus. I refused to say it. I refused to acknowledge it really happened.

By now I had thought about the question too much and tears began slowly dripping from my eyes. My brother hadn't said a word, and the doctor hadn't changed her expression at all. She just sat there patiently, trapping us with that composed gaze. I looked down at my shoes, knowing it would be easier to avoid conversation without the eye contact. The room remained silent. I had no intention to change that. Why would this lady care about what I would tell her anyway? When I walked out of her office she would put my files aside and proceed to question the next captive who sat down in the pleasantly comfortable chairs.

Finally my mom caved in and broke the perfect sounds of silence that filled the room. I don't blame her though. The poor doctor deserved some response. She was only trying to do her job. As my mom explained the events of December 8, everything from the leg pain to the blood clot to the house filled with relatives later that night, the doctor handed me a box of tissues. I took them grudgingly and simply grasped a few in my palm. What did I need her tissues for? Unless she could change what happened back in December, I had no use for her.

After almost an hour, our session ended. My brother and I walked out of the office full of heartache, but that was quickly overcome by our relief to be free. Once outside we took a deep breath of the crisp February air and began talking to each other.

At the time of the visit, I didn't realize that Emily had deliberately remained silent. I thought she just found it hard to talk to a stranger.

I felt a twang of relief when the doctor said, "The three of you are doing as well as can be expected," after talking to us. She ended the session with an invitation to return whenever the need arose. "Six weeks, six months, six years," she said.

The doctor was right on the last count. Six years later the confident face Em wore through her high school years faded. The cheerful countenance that bonded her, at first sight, to her first college roommate cracked

One mid-June afternoon, the office secretary buzzed my high school classroom. "Your daughter's on the phone."

"I'm on my way down." I placed the intercom phone receiver on its hook and headed straight to the office thinking *I wonder what's up.* Her finals were over. Em was back working at the summer ice cream stand she had been at since she was fifteen. In September she would return to college an upperclassman.

When I got to the office I picked up on line two.

"Hi Mom." Emily's voice sounded weak.

"You OK?" I asked.

"Yeah." The assertion was not convincing. "I'm better now."

"What's wrong.?"

"I just didn't feel too good." She paused. "So I called 911."

The calm facade I mustered up years ago, when Em left her tooth in her school desk, remained the stuff of light comedy. The composure I sought in this instance would have to conceal pure panic in a high drama of human struggle. I felt out of breath as my words got sucked into a nexus of angst.

"Oh my God Emily, what happened?"

"I felt like I couldn't breathe," she began. "Then my arm started to tingle."

"But you're all right now? What did the EMTs say?"

"Oh they're still here."

"Can I talk to one?" She put a paramedic on the phone.

"Hi. I'm Emily's mother. Is she OK?"

"She's fine Mrs. Hayden. Looks like she had an anxiety attack. But her vitals all check out fine now."

Her vitals? I thought. "An anxiety attack?" I had to repeat that aloud to grasp it.

"Yes, we suggest she follows up with her regular doctor in the next 24 hours."

I got home in ten minutes. The EMTs were gone. Em sat at the kitchen table, rubbing her arm. "I thought I was having an attack. Like Dad."

Emily had connected having trouble breathing with Larry having trouble breathing just before he died. Her fear – that she was home alone, dying – intensified the symptoms of an anxiety or panic attack, which mirror heart attack and pulmonary embolism symptoms: rapid breathing, shortness of breath, sometimes tingling or numbness in the left arm. Deciding what came first in this chicken-or-the-egg quandary determines treatment. Did anxiety cause Emily's shortness of breath (a likely panic attack) or did the shortness of breath cause the anxiety (possible heart or lung issues)? The paramedics had given her an EKG to be sure.

"You made the right choice, calling 911," I said, my voice trembling. I sat and my 20-year-old daughter folded onto my lap, her arms encircling my neck. We hugged and rocked like when she was a baby.

Emily made an appointment with our family doctor - who just happened to treat her former pediatrician, Dr. Gerry. That was how we chose our family doctor when Larry and I both turned forty and started to go for yearly physicals. If he was good enough for Doctor Gerry, he was good enough for us, and would be good enough for our children, when they outgrew a pediatrician.

The family doctor explained the differences between heart, lung, and anxiety issues and showed Emily how to breathe into a brown paper bag – a common remedy for hyperventilation. Yet, a tough summer lay ahead. Em had difficulty sleeping. She lost her *ommph,* lacked the spirit I always felt she acquired from her dad, a spirit immortalized on his Mazda RX7 license plate: ELAN 79. The registration tag still hangs below the front bumper of Emily's Corolla.

"She's just not herself," friends and family remarked. But I knew what she *was* – numb. I knew because I had been numb as well, ever since Larry died. I also went through the motions of being – a mime of existence – deliberate in movement, deadpan in mien. But I never covered it up with a smile, as she had. My numbness was a deadpan means of getting things done: the housework, the school papers, the lawn, the bills, the taxes.

Was my functional despondency contagious? I wished the psychologist had insisted we return sooner. Or that I had returned, alone. Maybe then, I would not have passed the malaise on to Emily by inadvertent example.

We worked hard at making her well that summer. Regular doctor checkups, healthful eating, yoga, and reading up on anxiety issues informed and encouraged us. Em sought counseling on campus when she returned to college in September – officially a child psychology major – an aspiration she also discussed in the college application essay about her first, discomforting session with a psychologist, a few years back. She closed the piece by saying:

> *If I could do it over again I don't know if I would talk. Ironically enough, I want to be a child psychologist*

when I grow up. I can't fully explain this decision after telling this story. I'll probably wind up in some teenage girl's English paper as a nameless meanie who asked the wrong question. Or maybe I won't. Maybe that was the most important day of my life because, in the midst of my silence, I discovered what I wanted to do for the rest of my life: sit children in comfy chairs and ask the right questions.

Which is exactly what Emily does these days as a child life specialist at Connecticut Children's Hospital, five years after the happy mask she had worn since shortly after her father's death simply wore out. "I meet the kids where they are at," she tells me. She draws with crayons beside children who have cancer, or puts puzzles together with sons and daughters whose siblings face a serious operation. Last summer she just listened to five cousins who needed to talk about a young patient who had died. "I got them to trust me first and then said, 'Let's talk about what happened,' That's not what the psychologist did with me."

I can't go as far as to say my daughter is cured of her sorrow. Grief is chronic, for sure, a disease the bereaved learn to live with for the rest of their lives, not shed. I still feel that I have to reel her in from a high and wide tide that rolls in, now and then, and separates us. Yet, its ebb always follows. Emily has learned to live with her loss – adjusted, I guess – and she continues to heal as her brother and I continue to heal. I wonder if she would have made healing others her life's work if Larry didn't die. Probably not.

Yet, two certainties do remain. One is how resilient she truly has been through her initial sorrow, her pretense of acceptance, her depression, and through the crises she faces at the hospital every day. The second, how she has made a mother – and father – so proud.

SLOW MOTION

Conor wasn't prepared to become the man of the house after Larry died. He was ready to have his father show him how to set screens on a basketball court. He was ready to follow the UConn Men's march to the Big East Championship in '99. The playoffs would have been Conor's first trip to Madison Square Garden with Larry, young follower and seasoned fan.

The hard year we had been through may have helped Conor tough it out, not that he had to be *tough*. Rough it out might be the better way to put it. Like roughing it on a camping trip. Doing without conveniences of home. Surviving without a father.

We had lost Piper, the Westie that had stood by me through a miscarriage and two pregnancies, in February '98. Fourteen years – almost 100 in doggie count – had taken its toll. Then we lost Larry's Dad in April, a massive heart attack. My children understood bad things can happen. But their father's death in December, when a blood clot traveled to his lung two weeks after heart surgery? That was way beyond bad.

Conor had been pretty resolute through other hurdles, starting as a baby. He was conceived on the Fourth of July, 1986, a year of extra special pyrotechnics, in honor of the Statue of Liberty centennial. Two months later the doctor joked as she calculated my due date. "Did you see fireworks?" We had. Fireworks and stars. Who knew that over time those stars would cross?

Pregnant with Conor just a year after Emily's birth, I hoped he would spare me the complications I had with Emily's C-section. I didn't want a second Caesarean. It wasn't that I felt robbed of the natural birth experience, as some women do, after the doctors cut a horizontal slit across my abdomen to birth Emily. Years of fertility counseling followed by a miscarriage left no room for regret after Em - a miracle child in my mind. But I didn't want to go through the five-day hospital stay that follows a C-section or the post-op pain killers. I wanted to get my newborn home to Big Sister as quickly as possible.

A month before I delivered Conor, an ultra-sound indicated normal weight and position.

"That gives you a 50-50 shot at a V-BAC," said the doctor. She used an acronym for vaginal birth after Caesarean. V-BACs were just becoming the exception to the "once a C-section, always a C-section" rule followed through my mother and grandmothers' child-bearing years.

When labor began, four weeks later, Larry kept me focused through a stop-and-go ride in morning rush-hour traffic to the hospital. "Just think *natural,*" he said as I kept track of the length of time between contractions.

"We can do this," he encouraged. I nodded, by then seated on the edge of a bed in the maternity ward just after my water broke. I tried to take a long, relaxing breath. I knew that each cramp would be tighter, stronger, and last longer than the previous one. I had gone through over a day of labor with Emily before the doctors called it quits and prepped me for surgery.

Larry took my hands into his. I blew out short, staccato breaths as I concentrated on one wave of contractions into the next. "Just think," he said. "No surgery. No pills." He continued his list of reasons for me to stay centered as I coughed and blew out *he he he he he he,* then louder and at a higher pitch, *HE HE HE HE, HE,* into his face, squeezing his hands, bluish under my white knuckles.

"What's so funny?" he joked. I wish I could have laughed.

No matter. He kept me on track through hours of contractions until the doctor appeared at my bedside and instructed me to push . . . PUSH . . . PUSH. We heard our son's first cry at 5 p.m. All of us had put in a full day's work.

"It could have gone either way," the doctor said when she discharged me the next morning. "You had some mighty fine coaching there."

In November 1988, over a year after Conor's birth, the American College of Obstetricians and Gynecologists officially declared new guidelines that allowed for more V-BACS, for the first time in 70 years. If Em was our miracle baby, Conor was our myth-buster.

His uncomplicated birth was an auspicious start - until we returned home. At once the myth-buster became a good-night's-sleep-buster with his day-in and day-out fussing. It didn't help that the dog thought the fretting sounded like an angry cat and retaliated with barks and nervous scampers. Baby Conor never slept more than twenty minutes at a time. After the umpteenth call to Dr. Gerry that week, he said, "If he hasn't settled in by now, it's likely colic."

Pediatricians often use the "Rule of Three" to diagnose colic: A baby that cries for three or more hours per day, at least three times per week, within a three month period. Conor doubled each count. Little can be done for the discomforting but otherwise, not serious condition, most often caused by an under-developed digestive tract that remedies itself over time. Breast milk or formula feeding makes no difference. Baby Mylanta drops and tummy massages do little to assuage the pain the baby feels.

After his colicky period, recurring ear infections interrupted Conor's sleep – again exacting more discomfort than a baby can tolerate without fussing the night away.

Over time, Larry and I also noticed that, during the day, Conor's speech wasn't connecting consistent sounds – like *wahf wahf* for the dog—the way Emily had at nine months. "*Daaa-dah,*" seemed to be his first word, to his father's delight, but soon after his first birthday Conor stopped saying even that. At eighteen months – when toddlers start to string sounds with a recognizable word or two – tests verified that ear infections had affected his hearing. This kept Conor from picking up audile clues for speech.

Shortly after, a simple surgery that inserts a barely visible drain into the middle ear ended Conor's cycle of pain. Within months he could say, "Aerostar go." One afternoon soon after, while sifting through a pile of Disney books with his four-year-old sister, Conor took *Pinocchio*, swung it overhead, and rammed the corner of the hard-cover volume into her face. She ran, screaming, into the kitchen, blood streaming from her nose. Conor followed behind, shouting. "*Paht kechup way Mama. Kechup way!*" At last he could utter a command, like most toddlers.

Immediately after Larry died, Emily and Conor began sleeping with me in the upstairs master bedroom. It was a grand room, an addition we had put on the small ranch by raising the roof two years earlier. Twice the size of our downstairs bedroom – which Emily took over – yet cozy. There was a TV and love seat on the east side and sliding doors that led to a high deck– where two could sit and wish on the stars before slipping into bed – on the west. When the renovation was complete, around our 17th anniversary, the children framed two handmade signs to decorate the new room. Em, eleven at the time, boldly printed NO KID ZONE over a splashy red, green, and yellow background. Conor, two years younger, drew the black outline of a smiley face – a little rough on the edges – and overlaid it with a thick red circle crossed by a diagonal line.

For a while after Larry died I would wake up facing the sliding door, turn over, still half-asleep, and reach out, expecting to find him by my side. The vacancy under my searching hand fully awakened me to the reality of missing him. There was some comfort, upon rising, to see Emily and Conor stretched out on air mattresses by my bed, still asleep, and in that moment, wrapped in their cartoon-character bedding, insulated from the reality of their loss.

In a week or so, as Christmas drew closer, we decorated the upstairs with tiny red poinsettia lights around the windows, a festive touch the children needed. On December 24 we watched what we always watched with Larry on that night - *Christmas Eve on Sesame Street.* The show was already twenty years old, and Mr. Hooper, the shopkeeper who saved the day in our favorite skit, had actually died before my children were born. Yet, there he was forever captured in the segment where Bert sells his paper clip collection to Mr. Hooper to buy Ernie a soap dish for his Rubber Duckie, and Ernie sells Rubber Duckie to Mr. Hooper to buy Bert a cigar box for his paper clip collection. As I watched Mr. Hooper return the prized possessions to the best buddies, in honor of their selflessness, I realized that Larry will always remain young and vital in my children's eyes. As my hair grays, my mind weakens, and my body fails, their memory of their father will always be the father they had when they were 11 and 13 years old.

Just after Christmas, Emily returned to her bedroom where she had more privacy and her own cordless phone. Conor stayed upstairs, even after he went back to school after the holiday break.

"You can stay up here with me as long as you need to," I told him early in the New Year.

"I'll stay to Valentine's Day," he said, surprising me with his quick, exact reply.

"As long as you need to," I repeated.

We never spoke about it again, but on February 13 I noticed his *Toy Story* blanket was missing from the upstairs room. His Buzz Lightyear toy was gone too. He had brought them downstairs and was busy tucking corners at the bottom of his bunk. Then he placed Buzz under those covers. On Valentine's Day morning he woke up in his own bed. His heartache, like his infant colic, was beginning to remedy itself.

Conor got past his colic and delayed speech the way the fabled tortoise outran the hare – slowly but steadily. He reminded us more of Ferdinand the Bull when he first stepped onto a soccer field.

"Where is he?" I would ask as dust settled around a pile of fumbling five-year-olds, all too young to have developed any finesse in the game.

"Over there." Larry would point to a quiet corner of the field where Conor sat picking dandelions. Once, he moseyed off a tad farther and sat on a swing in the playground by the field. He had twisted the chains above him and then lifted his feet. As his team made a goal, he spun in delight.

By second grade Conor started to bust chops on the soccer field. I remember the day I watched Larry and Conor through the kitchen window as one pair of large and one pair of small feet danced around the black and white ball. I heard Conor ask his father, "Who's your favorite painter?

The question took Larry by surprise, not so much for its content as for the context in which it was asked - just as the seven-year-old was about to steal the ball. The first three words, "who's your favorite," spilled out just as Conor stopped the moving ball, and pulled it back - out of his father's reach . The last word, "painter," popped out at the start of Conor's trademark two-step. An awesome move in which the boy seemed to step – with both feet – atop the ball, momentarily balance upon it and then aim his body and the ball a half turn away. In a flash, he dribbled the ball past his outwitted opponent.

"My favorite painter, hmmmm?" mused his father as he shook his head over the steal. "Sherwin Williams," he decided, raising one eyebrow as he spoke.

"Mine's Claude Monet," said Conor as he kicked the stitched sphere across the yard into a makeshift goal. His father's mouth gaped open in surprise.

How is it that an aspiring World Cup contender brings up a Nineteenth Century artist as nonchalantly as he might invoke Alexi Lalas - the Landon Donovan of the mid-nineties? I had a pretty good idea. When I helped out in his classroom earlier that week, I had noticed a hazy picture of sky, water, and rocks taped onto the blackboard by the window. *Afternoon on the Rhine* was printed in chalk above it; *Claude Monet 1840 to 1926, Impressionism,* below. The seven-year-old students were being introduced to the world of art appreciation.

Image and words had been absorbed by Conor's brain, ready to ooze out at any time - including a spontaneous backyard soccer spree.

"You know, Monet's one of my favorites too," Larry offered. He walked over to retrieve the ball. "In fact, there's a picture in Mom and Dad's room." He tossed the ball a short distance to his son. "It's a Monet print."

This time Conor's mouth fell agape. He dropped the soccer ball onto the grass, ran into the breezeway and then right passed me in the kitchen, down the hall to our bedroom. Sure enough, above the night table hung a print that seemed to emit its own light in the dark corner. A half dozen tiny white ducks swam in the foreground. Rippling circles bounced off the brood across shimmering green-gold waters. In the lower corner the signature *Claude Monet 74* identified the artist.

"Cool," said Conor. He saw the ducks and his father in a new light.

A few weeks later, I returned home from shopping to find father and son shooting hoops in the driveway. The random replay of Conor's young mind pitched another question his dad's way.

"Who's your favorite impressionist?"

Larry, who had his mind on the corner shot he was about to make from a chalk-drawn foul line, replied, rather automatically, "Rich Little." Neither of them heard me laugh.

"Mine's Andrew Wyeth," said Conor. He was thinking back to his second grade field trip to the Mead Museum on the Amherst College campus the day before. There he had seen Monet's original *Morning on the Seine, Giverny,* with its misty mood and lavender flavor, along with Hopper, Pollack, O'Keefe, and Wyeth paintings. It didn't matter that this young art critic had gotten his periods mixed up. From now on, the elegance in the arc of a basketball – on its trajectory to a rimless swish – would coexist in his mind with timeless objects of art. "I liked the way he painted lace curtains blowing through the window - just before the storm," Conor said. "They looked so real, like a photograph."

"They did, did they?" said his dad, watching the ball swish through the hoop. "You know Conor, we have to take a trip," he continued, retrieving the ball, going up for a shot, and missing. "There's a great art museum with lots of paintings - up at Williams College."

"Sherwin Williams?" asked Conor, going after the rebound.

Conor, Emily, Larry, and I continued through everyday dramas and reprieves. The extremes, mundane to out-of-the-ordinary, evened out to become our happily balanced, conventional life. In the first act, at least.

At times we crossed the line from commonplace to critical within minutes, even seconds. How well I remember the night Larry,

Emily, and I watched Conor teeter on this border in less time than it takes to zap a bag of popcorn. The scene could have played out in any home on our winding road that linked to neighboring towns on its north and south ends; a road where we joined a second generation of families, in what realtors call a bedroom suburb.

The ordinary summer afternoon had begun to sink into an ordinary summer evening. The bright August sky slipped away noticeably earlier than it had vanished a week ago. All four of us enjoyed these easy-going lapses before September stormed in with, if not real hurricanes, the high winds of return - to hectic grammar school and soccer schedules.

This evening we had, not unusually, grilled chicken on the outdoor barbecue. I put together an extra large tomato and basil salad – no lettuce – for this time of year. Still, it was impossible to keep up with the late garden harvest. By December I would be longing for August's fresh abundance, to no avail.

We took an after-supper swim in the backyard pool before twilight ushered in a sparkle of fireflies and the predictable presence of two bats flying lazy eights overhead, as they feasted on nighttime insects. The four of us latched onto this evening bliss the way summer ticks stick, embed, and nourish themselves onto their hosts - unnoticed.

The landscape darkened to mere shadows.

We headed indoors to watch Sunday night football, San Francisco at Jacksonville. Not a high stakes game – preseason. Besides, New England had kept a lead over their opponents through every quarter of the afternoon game – a match that *really* mattered to resident Patriots dichards.

"Want some popcorn?" I asked. As it was, Conor had already helped himself to an orange Popsicle out of the freezer. Sucking a frozen concoction suited his fascination with unusual noises.

Conor followed me back into the kitchen. As I put the *Jolly Time* bag into the microwave, I could see him out of the corner of my eye. He walked in circles, as restless nine-year-old boys do. He seemed intent on perfecting his recently acquired skill - belching at will.

"Quit it with the forced burps," I warned. At the same time, Emily and Larry joined us in the kitchen. Larry reached for bowls, large and small. More guttural noises ensued.

I looked straight at Conor now, and before I could grow more annoyed at the sound he was making, I became anxious. Something was wrong. I grabbed the largest bowl out of Larry's hands. Turned it to Conor. "Do you have to throw up?"

Conor kept pacing back and forth, but now he was gagging. He could barely utter, "I can't breathe," his face taut with terror.

As I shouted, "He can't breathe. He can't breathe," Larry dropped the smaller bowls onto the floor, steadied Conor from behind, and wrapped his arms around his son's waist. His left hand pressed the fist he formed with his right hand under Conor's rib cage. Larry pushed inward . . .upward. Once. Again.

The third squeeze dislodged a chunk of orange ice, slushy around the edges. The half-frozen lump flew across the kitchen floor like a failed field goal attempt.

Conor coughed a normal cough. He looked pale, but not blue. Startled. My arms joined Larry's, hugging the shaken boy.

"You're fine. You did great," I said.

I looked at Larry, then Em. "It's over."

I shut my eyes. The whole series of events brought me back twenty-five years to a day my grandfather began with his usual walk to get the *Daily News*. A typical day in which he clipped a few afternoon haircuts on the brick floor of his Brooklyn stoop (for my father's father was a retired barber). His routine continued through an ordinary evening, until he sat down to dinner with my grandmother and choked to death on a piece of lamb.

Beep. The kitchen microwave brought me back to my husband, daughter and son. The popcorn was done.

While Emily covered up her emotions shortly after her father died, Conor wore his grief on his sleeve. He seemed to go through the motions of doing his schoolwork. He ricocheted between periods of quietness and irritability. Once he told me a fellow sixth-grader had walked up to him in gym class and said, "My grandfather died last year. I don't see what the big deal is with your Dad." And Conor just walked away.

But there was anger, a seething he seemed to direct more toward himself. I'd see it after a bad soccer loss or a low test grade if my perception was right, though it may not have been. A child who loses a parent suffers the added liability of having a *grieving* surviving parent. Like the blind leading the blind. In a way, we had seeing-eye family and friends. A precious few that, after the funeral, the year anniversary, and over a decade of loss, didn't view Emily, Conor and I as objects of pity, but objects of their sincere affection and support instead.

The spring after Larry died Conor was chosen to speak at the sixth grade closing ceremony for D.A.R.E., the police officer-led curriculum that teaches children how to resist peer pressure, drugs, and violence. He stood before an auditorium full of parents, his classmates onstage behind him. "I have too good a life to waste with drugs or joining gangs," he said.

Too good a life? I questioned, until he went on to clarify. "Sure, I've had some things happen to me that I wish didn't. But if I thought drugs would help me get my mind off of that. I couldn't be more wrong. Drugs don't help your mind get over anything."

There was my son zeroing in on the dark gray opponent in the room – his grief – as if it was a soccer ball. He gingerly approached it, gauged his balance, and then took final aim by saying, "I feel good about myself, after things occurred that I wish didn't, by turning to my family and friends."

Conor became the man of the house through no choice of his own. Most of the time he and Emily were all the help I needed to get through household chores. Larry's brother, who delighted in calling me Crash after my unmanned Toyota rolled into my unmanned Aerostar in the driveway, said I could call him anytime. I told my children if I really needed to call Uncle Jeff, I would. But most of the time I didn't.

I had convinced myself that it wasn't so much I didn't want help. I'm just a do-it-now kind of person. Got that way growing up.

Whenever I'd say, "I have homework," my mother would say, "Do it now." I'd put off practicing the accordion or cleaning my room and she'd repeat, "Do it now."

So *now*, when I notice, one morning, how dry and splintery the deck's become, I hose it down and get in the car to head to Home Depot while it dries. I pick up a couple of cans of wood stain and sealer – I prefer to overbuy rather than have to go back for more – and have the first coat applied in time for a late lunch.

One rainy afternoon when Conor was around, I got the idea to move a bookcase so I could wash the vinyl wallpaper in the entire hallway - not just the exposed walls.

"Help me move the bookcase?" I asked.

"Sure." He walked over to start to unload a shelf.

"You don't have to do that. We'll just slide it," I said.

"I don't know, Mom."

"Let's just try."

We started to slide, or better said – inch - the six foot bookcase. It was loaded with a full set of *The World Book Encyclopedia,* circa 1957, a gently used collection of *Sesame Street Treasury Books* (bought one volume a week at the supermarket), years of *Ranger Rick* magazines, months of *Time,* and a single copy of every book in my high school English curriculum. We got halfway through the doorway to Conor's room when the bookcase began to tip. I caught it, but wound up wedged against the bedroom door. Even though the bookcase remained standing, at a most precarious angle, the books and magazines poured onto the floor in a heap of soft-and-hard-cover rubble.

"Oh no," I sighed. "Are you OK?" Conor steadied the empty bookcase and then reached out to help guide me out of my predicament.

"Is it time to call Uncle Jeff yet?" was all he said.

His voice of reason halted me. It sounded like the good sense his father would make whenever I lost mine. Like when Larry would say,

"Don't worry if the house isn't perfect - you work full time," after I fretted over unexpected company.

Or, "The family isn't going to fall apart if you don't make your Easter bread this year," after a self-imposed guilt trip.

And even, "She's just a kid - you expect too much from her," through a mother-daughter impasse.

Now, thirteen-year-old Conor, the toddler who couldn't talk, was speaking for himself and, sort of, for his Dad. Perfect timing too. Em was in high school. She craved more freedom, a later curfew. "I think you're being too hard on her," Conor told me after one rant and rave.

And then, "I think you need to let up a bit on yourself too Ma."

I wonder if there are humor chromosomes scientists haven't discovered yet. Little pieces of coiled DNA that pass on the ability to turn a phrase, juxtapose wit with wisdom.

Larry had a way with words. Every year, never fail, his entry would be recognized in the *Journal Inquirer's* annual St. Patrick's Day limerick contest. I'd say he was most pleased with his 1995 entry.

> *At the drive - in he tried to explore*
> *Rebuffed, he could only implore*
> *If it isn't too late*
> *Could I have one more date?*
> *Like the Raven she quoth: "Nevermore."*

The feature editor commented that it was one of the few entries that captured the "bad boys in the back of the room," tradition of the genre. Larry liked that, even though he was really one of the good guys who sat front row, center.

Conor absorbed his father's wise nature (in both senses of the word) before his father died - or it was in his genes. Larry's brothers, in their fifties and sixties now, pull me aside and say, "He's turned into Larry." The likeness they see transcends his father's tall, thin frame and thick head of hair. Conor is athletic, like Larry, and he possesses not only the agility to play the sport, but the fluency to analyze it the way his father did.

As I think about this Conor is on his way to attend the 2010 Alabama vs. South Carolina game with his cousin and Uncle Jim. It's a first big-time college game trip for Jim and his son. Conor started his own tradition to witness this level of football two years ago, when he drove out to Michigan State one weekend and Penn State, another, blogging the experiences.

I received a text message from Conor, from over 800 miles away, just minutes ago.

> *beer brats burgers & gameday playing in the background - this is heaven*

I'm not surprised by his delight and I know this pilgrimage is not only about the win - though he'd really like to see the underdog Gamecocks hold back the Crimson Tide in this afternoon's game.

(another text rolls in : *Im 20 ft behind the stage*)

I turn ESPN on and see a sea of heads behind the sports correspondents seated on a portable platform. I'm thrilled knowing Conor is one of those fans.

How do I know it's not only about the win? Last year, when Conor attended Penn State's rout of his beloved Michigan he blogged:

> *The game was a cold, rainy blowout in which an over-matched and out-classed Michigan team did everything in its power to take all the life out of the home stadium.*

When I read his October, 2009 blog, I noticed he filtered Michigan's 35-10 loss through another lens.

> *Say what you want about it, there is something to be said for Michigan fans clapping and fist pumping as they proudly sang "Hail to the Victors" long into the fourth quarter of a game that had long since been decided. Yes, thousands of the lesser fans had started to disperse out of the stadium as early as the third quarter,*

> *and I make no judgment of that decision. But the true
> fans, the ones who get it, remained. And I am proud to
> say, I was one of them.*

Conor has never read the essay Larry wrote in college, simply titled, "The Fan." He hasn't because I had misplaced it. I remember having it in my hands years ago, and had been looking high and low for it ever since.

I found it one morning this week in the bedroom nightstand, the drawers of which I hadn't opened for years. I had forgotten that the essay was handwritten. I thought it had been typed along with Larry's other college papers. But then, some of the pieces of his undergraduate work saved with it were typed on almost transparent onion-skin paper, and some were scribed in his flowing longhand. How some things have changed and how some things haven't, I think as I now go back to reread Larry's last paragraph.

> *The good fan is obsessively victory-oriented. This
> singlemindedness of character makes the fan the eternal
> optimist. For although he may be crushed in defeat to-
> day, he will surely return equally optimistic tomorrow.*

Why does that sound so much more like a survival tactic against losing than rooting and tooting? Because the fan is a survivor - of the best and of the worst team play. As Larry wrote:

> *Whatever virtues the fan professes to hold, charity is
> not one of them, for the fan is best able to express his
> sentiment when he is in his ugliest mood.*

Conor may have lost his father at age 11, but, at 23, he has acquired his keen ways of seeing and being.

I am shaking as I read Larry's words. Crying too, but with more gladness of heart than aching. South Carolina is ahead 21- 3 in the second quarter. I know my son is elated. I want to sit back and share the rest of the game with him today. I'll give the young fan his father's essay when I see him on Monday.

MOVING

I see a pony-tailed, bearded, craggy-faced Irishman standing in front of Smyth's Soft Serve Ice Cream Stand. I am pretty damn sure it is him. And he seems to be looking my way as if he is pretty damn sure it is me.

I approach the ice cream window but can't resist a second sidelong glance. That does it. His eyes stand out like bright blue dinghies against a gray and furrowed Killarney shore.

I speak first. "Do you know me?"

And there it is. The deep and hearty laugh I remember so well. "Ah-ha, ah-ha, ah-ha. I think so."

Tom and I go back over forty years. A high school friend of my twin brother (also named Larry), Tom would call him "Laura's brother" and me "Larry's sister." Class musician. Played a mean horn in the pit when the Lamplighters put on *Oklahoma* in '67. The *Courant* ran a front page picture of Tom playing the trumpet in the Hartford Symphony during a performance of *Aida,* a year or so later.

But in the early Seventies, low draft numbers that were based on a young man's birth date superseded well-laid plans. Tom won this lottery – one I knew nobody wanted to collect on – and had to swap his orchestra rank to one in the U.S. Navy. Seaman Apprentice Thomas Conley shipped for Vietnam a year before he would have completed his part-time degree at the Hartt College of Music.

Tom attended my brother's wedding just before he headed to Vietnam in '71. I hadn't seen him since we graduated from high school. We caught up during my visit to a table filled with my brother's high school buddies. "I'll start teaching in town in a few weeks," I told him.

"Be on the lookout for my little brother. A hellion," he cracked and drew a laugh deep from his Irishman's belly. A laugh that could brighten the dark side of the moon.

We agreed to keep in touch.

In the Seventies, late bloomers like me were better at letter writing than the *real good lovin'* the Rascals sang about. Sex, drugs, and rock and roll for some of us were more like college mixers with boys from Providence College (bused in at six and out at ten), a bottle of Thunderbird wine (Matues for special occasions), and the Judy Collins version of "Both Sides Now." Like the lyrics to the song, I really didn't know love at all.

So I wrote letters.

And he wrote back: *Dear Larry's Sister* . . . followed by mostly small talk. A stick figure or two in the margin. Fun stuff.

At first I would get as many letters as I sent. Then two to my one. Then none.

My last letter to Tom began: Dear Tom-*ass*, followed by:

> Sorry,
> slip of the mind
> that salutation.
> Just
> so low and bitchy and
> if I dare
> read this again
> I'll probably mail it
> never.

I did read the fumbling verse again. I never did send it. But it really wasn't a big deal - more word-play on my part than foul play on his. We didn't have a serious relationship. He was my brother's friend. I was his friend's sister.

And so it goes, as Vonnegut's anti-war fantasy told us in those days.

Tom didn't call me Larry's sister when we ran into each other at the ice cream stand, but we dwelled on what my brother was up to.

"He still at Berklee?" Tom asked.

"Head of the guitar department," I said. The irony didn't escape me. Here I was talking to my high school Class Musician about my twin who had become a successful guitarist. The discrepancy played out even further. Tom and Larry both had low draft numbers in '71, but Larry enlisted in the Army before the draft got him. Enlistees had a chance at special duties and his music degree gave him a shot at an audition for a military band. The stateside Army band. For Larry, it was a risk worth taking. Shortly after Tom shipped off to Saigon, Larry got stationed in D.C. with the twenty-piece U.S. Army Strolling Strings. While Tom worked on Navy electronics, overseas, Larry played Nixon dinner parties. Gave guitar lessons to General Westmoreland's son.

"His music is his life," I said. "And his four kids."

"One hell of a guitarist," said Tom.

When the conversation turned to me, I condensed a quarter-century of joy and sorrow in two sentences. "I'm busy raising my daughter and son. My husband died four years ago." I spared him the rote script I had repeated so many times since a blood clot traveled to my husband's lung two weeks after successful heart surgery, killing him instantly.

His voice dropped. "I'm sorry." He hesitated. "I brought my daughter up alone. Her mother died when she was five."

I may have known that. Bad news travels wide and deep in the suburbs. But it had never been news I trusted or had time for, in a solid marriage and family.

"Kim's graduating from Clarkson next month," he said. I could tell he was proud of her – and his – accomplishment.

We decided I would invite my brother to my house for dinner with Tom there. I could bake lasagna and fry an eggplant. They could talk about my brother's early days at Berklee.

A week later, between appetizer, entrée, and dessert, I heard about *Freeway,* Tom's defunct rock band with Dennis, another high school musician, his bartending days at Bradley Airport's

Terrace Room, the Eighties manufacturing layoffs, and wood-craft, his new trade.

"You won't believe who came into the shop last week," Tom said after dinner, referring to the woodworking store he managed. "Diane."

"No kidding?" my brother said. "The only soprano who's sung the lead to *Oklahoma* with an English accent. And how's Pete doing?"

"They're not together anymore. She's remarried," said Tom.

"Who would've figured?"

Tom stuck around for a while after Larry left. We weren't into old times. We talked about my present and his more recent past: raising children who had lost a parent. Why my home had pictures of my husband on every wall, and how they couldn't even be rearranged without one of the kids asking, *Whatcha do with Dad's picture?*

Two months later Tom joined the children and me on the Connecticut shore for a day. We played miniature golf together. A week later they met Peggy, his favorite aunt who guarded the family's secret Irish soda bread recipe from every niece and nephew - except Tom.

In time we were a couple. Not a traditional couple. A couple of survivors. Survivors who understand that the needs of kids who suffer loss come before the needs of adults who suffer loss. Survivors who still have to eke out a living and take care of their own selves. Survivors who can help realign the planets in each others' universe.

I asked Tom about why he had stopped writing back, years ago.

"'Nam does a job on you," he said, looking downward. I noticed he was speaking in the present tense. "Letters from home are what keep you going. They remind you of the people you need to know care about you. The places you need to get back to." He paused, then finished, looking straight at me now. "It was too hard to write back about what was going on there."

As fall approached I asked Tom, "What would you think of signing up for ballroom dancing lessons?" A beginner's class was starting at one of the schools through the evening adult education program.

"We could give it a try," he said.

I am learning to waltz with Tom, a musician, a man who understands rhythm. We triple step up and down the school cafeteria floor the first night of Al's Ballroom dance class. Tom emphasizes the initial step of each cluster with ease as he steps forward:

ONE- two-three, ONE-two-three.

His right hand touches my back, just under my shoulder. His left palm is in my right palm, shoulder high.

I step to the rear to, it seems, the pulse of an alternative heartbeat:

LUB-dub-dub, LUB-dub-dub.

I attempt to do what Ginger did with Fred – every move backwards and in heels. This is no time for abandon. Ballroom dancers need to stay on their feet, not get swept off them. We do not want to hurt ourselves.

When I was eight I'd pranced around the parlor stereo – solo – to Gwen Verdon singing *Ven Vi Valtz*, from the Fifties Broadway musical *New Girl in Town*. The beat would work its mellow way through the *yumpy dumpy dump* refrain only if I started the first *Ven vi* on the off beat, placing the accented step on VALTZ, like so:

Ven vi VALTZ – yumpy dumpy DUMP
Ven vi VALTZ – yumpy dumpy DUMP
Ven vi VALTZ – Ven vi VALTZ – We're the BESTest

Much to Tom's surprise, I know a bit about rhythm too.

Our six-week course on the waltz, fox trot and swing extended to another six weeks at the instructor's studio. Session two introduced the Latin dances. When that ended the class actually talked the instructor into another six weeks, and then another, and another, for going on eight years now. An oasis right smack in the middle of hundreds of work weeks.

My children outgrew the backyard pool, single beds, and their penchant for freezing time. They moved on to college, their own apartments, adorned their own spaces. The home we once shared began to echo the hollow sounds of mere memory and me.

I decided to look for someplace smaller.

I wasn't planning to move two miles from Tom. Ten miles between us had worked just fine. We had our mid-week dance lesson and monthly weekend dance - our time-outs between his six-day work week in retail and my round-the-clock cycle, teaching by day and correcting by night. The realtor suggested I consider looking at a house in the next town over, just walking distance to the small ranch where Tom had raised his daughter and built his woodshop. I chuckled to myself. What harm could there be in looking?

I liked my realtor. He had been a student at the high school where I taught. Had a learning disability in math. I could tell when he drew up the contract for the house. He'd punch the calculator over and over and ask me, "Is that right?"

I only once caught an error.

What he lacked in math skills he compensated for in people skills. His gently paced persuasion began as he unlocked the back door of the tiny cape.

"Note the charm in the wainscoting," he said as his hand followed the freshly painted ledge that surrounded the room.

I did, all the while thinking *is this too close? Too close to Tom?*

"Big kitchen for a small home," he continued. I nodded, loving the idea of a roomy kitchen in a downsized house. *But what if Tom doesn't go for the idea?*

"Laundry room's there on the right."

My head shook in surprise. I could not hide my delight over this bright enclosure with washer and dryer hook-ups, a mere step off of the dine-in kitchen. I wouldn't have to go up and down the basement stairs to wash clothes.

But would moving closer to Tom drive him away? A stubborn Irishman of few words, he liked his own space. Believed purging the demons of loss and war to be solitary work.

The realtor opened the window. The scent of wisteria wafted into the room.

"It's small, in perfect condition. And the taxes are low because of the airport," he continued as we walked across the hardwood floor in the dining room.

"What about noise?" I asked, searching for a drawback.

"Flight patterns take the planes over Suffield. You won't hear a thing."

He seemed to have the right answer for every question.

"Let's take a look at the porch," he said, leading me to the front end of the house. The living room glowed in the late afternoon sun.

I stepped through the door onto the cozy covered entrance that faced the side yard. At once, I could picture flower boxes filled with geraniums and trailing ivy atop the porch's waist-high walls. A cushioned rocker in the corner by the door. A table for two at the center.

I didn't know it yet, but I was sold. I just couldn't own up to it that soon. Too busy looking for reasons *not* to buy this house. Too involved, the next day and day after that, driving up and down its street at all hours of the night, on the lookout for anything remotely suspicious. I even called the police department.

"Hello. I'm looking at a house on Silver Lane," I told the officer. "Could you tell me if you get much , er, activity there?"

"Where?" he asked.

"Silver Lane," I repeated.

"Can't say I even know where that is."

"A dead end off of Center, just a few blocks up from Elm," I told him, glad I had cased the neighborhood.

"Elm? Why lady, you're right in our backyard. No problems there."

Right – no problem, except that 15 Silver Lane, built in the nineteenth century, refurbished in the twenty-first, just happened to be located two miles from Tom. The Broadway soundtrack of my youth played again in my head. Sammy Davis Jr. singing *Too Close For Comfort* in *Mr. Wonderful*. A fox trot.

I had to talk to Tom. Be straight with him. I wouldn't be asking any more from him. Just less distance. No, no, bad wording. I'd go another route. Try to keep it light.

The next Wednesday night we danced. I brewed Starbuck's dark Italian Roast at home afterward, as I always do, and then, somewhere between talking about an Olbermann editorial and the latest Knofler CD, popped the question:

"Would you feel as if I was stalking you if I moved to Windsor Locks?"

He laughed that laugh that first drew me to his heart and said, "Wouldn't bother me."

I wasn't planning on buying a house two miles from Tom's house. I wasn't planning on my husband dying either. I wasn't planning on stopping to get an ice cream the day Tom was getting an ice cream or "Fumbling into Ecstasy" with him to the Sarah McLachlan song. The two men in my life have taught me not to plan on anything.

And so it goes.

MANTRA

U ntil my appointment with a urologist one July afternoon, I had played mind over matter about the results of my regular physical the week before. I felt fine. Perhaps more tired than usual, but the school year had just ended with its correcting triathlon of research papers, writing portfolios, and final exams. Five high school classes - assessed, recorded, and calculated into final grades in less than a week. Every year I joked that if the mental exercise of this annual grind was physical, English teachers would go into cardiac arrest from the sudden switch of too much schoolwork to no work at all. There was no cool down period.

I expected to go to my yearly exam and not have to see the doctor again until next summer. Instead, I got a phone call the next day.

"There are traces of blood in your urine and your liver function is off," he told me. "We've got to find out why."

"But I feel fine," I said.

"That's a good sign, but I want to rule out the worst first," he continued. "I'm scheduling you for tests Monday and a follow-up with a urologist."

After my husband's death, five years earlier, I would think *where is Larry when I need him* whenever a crisis unraveled. I could have used his help the night the '90 Corolla totaled the '88 Aerostar. It was just months after he died. *He* would have put the car in park after pulling into the garage. After we carried grocery bag after grocery bag into the kitchen, *he* would have been sure to press the button by the entrance to shut the automatic garage door. That way, even if the car was not in park and started to roll back down the

ever-so-slightly inclined cement floor – it would have been stopped
by an easy bump.

But I didn't shift into park or close the door. While Emily and
Conor helped put groceries away, the Toyota continued to creep
backwards onto the top of our steep curved driveway. The back
wheels picked up speed on the asphalt slope and – without a driver
to steer through the S-curve of the paved surface – tore straight over
the early spring grass and onto the side lot where the van was parked.
As the children and I finished packing produce into the fridge, we
heard a crash.

Conor got to the dining room window first and fanned open the
heavy drapes.

"Whooooa," he said, in typical sixth-grade fashion.

Emily, two years older, got more specific. "The car hit the van."

"What the. . ." I began.

I shut my eyes. I couldn't bear to look at how the car's back bumper smashed into the middle of the van's sliding passenger door. I
thought *where is Larry when I need him,* my head twisting side to
side. I forced myself to peer through the pane again. I realized it
could have been worse than an empty family car totaling an empty
family van. Had the long tan Aerostar not stopped the silver gray
Corolla, the car would have rolled onto the road, possibly hitting an
oncoming vehicle.

Where was Larry when I needed him? I wondered one night the
next winter as Emily kept throwing up a chalky antibiotic prescribed
to fight pneumonia. I ached for Larry's help at the start of the next
school year - when I could do little more than hand Conor the "really
big towel" he asked to bring to school for his first gang shower in
seventh-grade gym class.

The day I shouted, "Where the hell are you when I need you
most," I was alone in the Windstar that had replaced the van, crying.
At a stoplight I tried to shake an unyielding steering wheel amid my
rant and tears. Like most days, I was in the throes of one unrelenting
charge after another: houseclean, food shop, vacuum pool, shower,
visit Mom, see doctor, and pick up Conor for a soccer game an hour
away.

It was the doctor's visit that unnerved me, the urologist my regular doctor had sent me to – that July afternoon – just before picking up Conor for a preseason high school match. That was when I found out "feeling fine" is not necessarily an indication of one's true health.

The urologist spoke matter-of-factly in front of a backlit X-ray screen.

"These are your kidneys." He pointed to a pair of smudges on what looked like an illuminated Rorschach test to me. I nodded.

"See this?" He pointed to a shadow behind one of the smudges. "That shouldn't be there."

Then he tightly folded the fingers of his right hand into his palm and said "This is your right kidney - about the size of a human fist." He made another fist with his left hand, this one looser than the first. He placed the left fist atop his right and said, "This is the tumor growing on your kidney. The tumor is slightly larger."

But I felt fine. I hadn't experienced any pain. There was no perceptible bleeding. No lump either. Just a shadow behind a smudge.

I remembered the shadow on my father's X-ray – thirteen years earlier. A shadow that appeared six months before he died of lung cancer.

Dad was a smoker all his life – or at least up to the heart attack he suffered when I was pregnant with Emily. The morning after he had gotten through a critical night, the doctor asked him if he smoked. Dad looked at the monitors that charted his heartbeat, breathing and blood pressure, then at Mom and me – with my swelled belly. "Not anymore," he said. The resolution bought him some time, but after five years his "smoker's cough" worsened, even though he hadn't had a cigarette since the heart attack. When a shadow appeared on his X-ray, he was diagnosed with lung cancer and began radiation and chemotherapy. But ten years ago, by the time an X-ray confirmed lung cancer, treatment merely postponed the inevitable.

My doctor's voice brought me back to the present. "With this kind of kidney cancer, we remove the tumor and the kidney. Lessens the risk of recurrence." Then he added, "Patients adjust to one kidney quite well."

I was still trying to adjust to the fact that from one afternoon errand to the other, I had become a cancer patient facing major surgery. A cancer patient with a demanding job, an aging mother, and more important than anything else, a cancer patient with two children who had lost their father to complications after his heart surgery four years earlier.

Having to lose a kidney scared the shit out of me. Maybe it was shock, maybe it was denial, but I remained pretty steady in the doctor's office. I was circumspect as I made my pre-op appointment at the desk, not emotional. Confirmed that Emily and Conor could come if they had any questions.

The tears and jeers came at the red light, on the way to pick up Conor. *"Where the hell are you Larry? How am I going to get through this one without you?"* A driver in the next lane looked at me as the light changed to green. I gave my head a shake the way a dog does rousing from a nap. Took a deep breath. Regulated my breathing as the Windstar accelerated to 10 . . . 20 . . . 30 mph. I was steadier now, on my way to Conor. We'd soon be headed an hour south to his game. I would wait to tell him what lay ahead until we returned and his sister got home from working at a local ice cream stand.

Bzzzzzzzz, Bzzzzzzzzz. My phone vibrated in the cup holder on the Windstar console. I pressed the green button, heard my twin brother's voice calling from Boston. He knew about the appointment.

"Bad news," I said. "I have cancer. I'm going to lose a kidney."

"Lose a kidney? Are they sure? You going to see another doctor?"

"I saw the tumor. It's bigger than the freakin' kidney. My primary care doctor says this guy's the best. "

My brother didn't know what to say. He was having his own problems. The health issues men in their mid-fifties often experience had led to a number of biopsies of his prostate. Nerve wracking, but not life-threatening. Not cancer.

"I can't talk now. I'm on my way to pick up Conor. We're going to his soccer game."

I was relieved not to have to hang out with the town Moms at the game. Nancy, my long-time high school friend, met me on the away team's field that ran just below the Amtrak line to New Haven. She had moved to the southern part of the state years ago.

The week before the game Nancy had driven up for lunch with me and two other girlfriends – Cindy and Marilyn. Our annual get-together. The four of us had attended each other's weddings, baby showers, and three of our fathers' funerals. They were the friends I felt the most comforted by when Larry died. Knew him since high school. Worked the summer playgrounds with him. Cindy even dated Larry for a short time out of high school – until she broke it off.

Just last summer Marilyn helped me paint my dining room a soothing lilac. She talked me into replacing the drapes with maroon and ecru sheers wrapped loosely around corner holdbacks. My concert buddy, we've sung along in the bleachers to Fogerty, Mellencamp, Dylan, and Young while sending picture messages to our kids.

How quickly, it seemed, we four had turned thirty, forty, and now over fifty together. These women are my adult lifelines.

"It'll be fine," Nancy said at our lunch date, before we ordered. "They have to check everything now. Malpractice you know." We chatted, lingered, and even asked the waitress to take our picture. "Old bitties luncheon," we joked.

Nancy met me the evening of Conor's soccer game dressed as impeccably as in her high school days: navy Bermuda shorts, white Izod shirt, and a sweater draped over her shoulders. She hadn't been at that field since her son played – three or four years earlier.

"How'd it go?" she asked.

"Not good." I answered. She held my hand as I told her about the smudges, the shadow, and the operation. "They're gonna take out the kidney too." I said.

"That's OK. Believe me. Andrew has only one kidney." She spoke of her son.

"Why? What happened?"

"Oh nothing happened. He was just born with one. We didn't even know until he had appendicitis a few years ago. When they gave him an ultrasound for that – they noticed he had only one kidney. Otherwise we might have never known."

"Really," I said.

Good news travels. Bad new flies nonstop. Within a few days of mailing my official request for a two-month medical leave from my teaching job, I got a phone call from Sarah – another high school friend.

"Laura," she said with a noticeable heaviness in her voice. "I heard."

"What did you hear?"

"Terry called me." Terry had graduated with us too. Now she cleaned Emily and Conor's teeth at a dentist office in town. "They read your letter at the Board of Education meeting last night."

"In closed session, right?"

"I know, but Ter's son's on the Board. I hope you don't mind me calling."

"Well no. I'm still trying to get use to the news myself." I gave her my short version of the spots, the smudges, and the shadow drama that was playing out in my body.

"I want to help," she said. "I want to work on you."

"Work *what* on me?"

"Consegrity."

Sarah is, was, and always will be a dearly intense friend. A dark-headed beauty, she represented our hometown in a state beauty pageant after high school graduation. When she worked for a Fortune 500 company she seemed to spend more time in the air than on the ground. Now she was practicing the healing art.

"I can come there or do it long-distance," she said.

"You can?" I was fascinated.

"It's best if you are resting."

"I see."

Sarah explained, in almost textbook fashion, consegrity therapy. Practitioners locate energy blockages in cells and connective tissues. The treatment removes these obstructions so that the cells and connective tissues can return to their innate ability to withstand tension and stress.

Since Larry died, tension and stress seemed part of my daily routine. I began to resent the expression friends and relatives frequently tossed my way. "Your plate is so full," they would say. As if I should go on a responsibility diet. What could I cut down on? My kids? My job? My aging Mom, who was exhibiting more and more signs of increased anxiety and confusion? My grief? I had more energy blockages than a corroded car battery. And here was Sarah offering me a way to strengthen the circuitry, get the gunk out.

"I don't even have to touch you," she said.

I accepted Sarah's offer using the same rationale from a 1970s philosophy course that convinced me to believe in God: Pascal's Wager Argument. Even though the consegrity cure, like the existence of God, could not be proven, I'd be wise to bet on it – for consegrity, like faith, would encourage healthy behaviors. Nothing to lose, serenity to gain. Even my doctor agreed the sessions could do no harm - as long as the alternative therapy didn't interfere with the traditional treatment of Stage Two kidney cancer: get the fucker out now!

I can't say I got much from the long-distance treatment except extra time in bed. On a couple of designated days Sarah instructed me to lie still before getting up in the morning, so she could start working on me from her home at the same time - a half hour away. She had a hectic schedule energy- healing other patients and moving her organic foods business along. I found myself with less free time than ever focusing on Emily and Conor's activities, getting Mom through my ordeal, writing lesson plans for my substitute teacher, keeping doctor appointments and, as they say, getting my affairs in order – just in case, as with Larry, the cure became tragically worse than the disease.

On the day Sarah arrived at my home for a face-to-face session, late-afternoon sun sparkled across the backyard pool and into the windows facing west. My mother and mother-in-law visited outside through my hour therapy. Patient and practitioner were not to be disturbed.

Sarah's soft gauzy top and loose cotton shorts seemed to float on her as she drew the curtains. Her long black hair twisted in a messy bun.

"You have to relax, close your eyes, sleep if you want to," she told me as she opened a three-ring binder across the floor and positioned herself erect on the striped loveseat, looking down on the notebook. I welcomed the opportunity to stretch out on the couch, slow the pace of the day, shut my eyes. And I peeked, even though Sarah told me not to. Saw her flip pages back and forth, tap her thigh, and shut her eyes, immersed in the business of healing.

I began to drift off to somewhere between earth and space, reality and reverie, fear and forgiveness. In the stillness I started to mentally recite the rosary as I habitually do just before falling asleep and just after awakening. Then moved from rote prayer to petition, but not to God. *Stay with me Larry, with me and the kids. We need you so badly. So very badly.* For the next half hour, I slept more peacefully than I had in years. A penetrating sleep in the pursuit of wellness. I awoke energized. Hopeful.

Two days before the operation, Sarah called.

Laura, I have terrific news. "I've been working on you from here," she paused, but her sentence didn't sound finished. I waited.

". . . and it's gone."

"What's gone?" I asked.

"The cancer's gone."

"Sarah, the operation's the day after tomorrow."

"But you don't *need* the operation."

I didn't understand. Even after she explained how my energy was clean, my charts - clear, the disease- gone, I didn't get it. I couldn't get it.

"Talk to your doctor, Laura," she said.

I had more than due respect for Sarah. I felt due love - for the gift of tranquility she had passed onto me that sunny afternoon. But, tell my doctor – a doctor who, thank God, detected a malignancy before it was too late – tell him to cancel?

I had to say, "I can't tell the doctor to call off the operation Sarah."

"Just tell him you want a CT-scan – today. He'll see you don't need the operation."

My life was at stake on this wager. So were my faith in my doctor and his faith in me. I stacked my chips on the operating table.

The phone rang again. This time it was Cindy.

"Thought I'd check in," she said.

"Glad you did." Of all the girls, I felt most connected to Cindy. Her Mom called me "the fourth daughter." The sisters hosted a Sweet Sixteen surprise party for me in their cellar and introduced me to Cape Cod. Ten years after high school graduation, when I started dating Larry, the oldest joked, "Cindy let a good one get away there."

"You don't sound so good," she said.

"Getting nervous."

"Well, I was going to wait to tomorrow to call. But I had a dream last night – about Larry."

"You did?" How I longed to dream about Larry again. I did a few times back. Always a confusing scenario – a Mexican restaurant with checkered tablecloths once – where I'd reach down to pick up something – a napkin – and when I'd sit up again, he'd be gone. Vanished into thin air.

"He told me to tell you everything is going to be all right."

"Oh my God, he said that?" I was crying now. Cindy was as a-matter-of-fact friend as you could get. What you saw in her life – devotion to her husband and son, an uncanny connection to animals – was what you got. I had only one question as I regulated my breathing to speak. "But why did he tell you and not me?"

"He said he tried to tell you."

"Tried?"

"Maybe you were closed to his message."

Maybe I was too busy.

Two days later my brother traveled from Boston to take me to the hospital. I told him about both phone conversations on the way. I stayed strong, really strong during prep at the hospital - even joked to the anesthesiologist, "I don't usually introduce myself to men lying flat on my back." But when the nurses wheeled me into the operating room – the whitest, shiniest room I have ever seen – and I saw a line of sharp stainless steel instruments ready to be used to cut a seven-inch incision – I lost it. I sobbed like a baby in that nurse's arms as she said, "Everything is going to be all right," over and over until the anesthesia took full effect.

Twelve hours later my brother met me in my hospital room. Still woozy, I asked, "Did you call the kids."

I called the whole list," he said. "Told almost everyone you did fine."

"Almost everyone?" I was confused.

"Yeah. Left Sarah the message: 'They took the tumor out'"

The next day the surgeon told me he removed a mass that weighed over eight ounces. Less than half was my kidney. The rest was an abnormal growth that spread seven centimeters across.

"The tumor looked good," he said. "Malignant, but encapsulated. The toxicology report should confirm that next week."

After the surgeon left I swallowed two white pills for the pain on my right side. I pressed the remote that turned on a TV shelved near the ceiling and switched to the Relaxation Channel. *Sarah would be pleased* I thought as I recalled the way she helped me slow my pace through the chaos of the previous weeks. I don't know what motivated her to suggest I didn't need the operation. But I never considered foregoing the surgery - not for a second. I wasn't in the market for a miracle. Just a surgeon I could trust from the day I was diagnosed through the day of the operation.

From now on, barring an ugly twist of fate – like Larry's clot– I will have to manage my own wellness. Get back on my feet. Go for X-rays.

I'll slow down a bit too. Keep my head and heart attuned to forces of life - and death. Become more mindful of Larry. He's closer than I thought.

On the screen above I watched calm waves break to a soothing foam against an uninhabited shore. As my ache subsided, the TV appeared to turn somersaults in my direction, but I fell asleep before the tumbling set could reach me.

FIGMENTS

Early in his remarkable essay "Chimera," Gerald N. Callahan, a professor of immunology at Colorado State University, grapples with the loss of his wife, and the odd occurrence of, what seems to him, her reappearance. If I were to paraphrase the start of his essay to mirror my experience, I would write:

Last Monday, one of those drab early December days when mostly chickadees skitter upon weather-worn bird feeders, my husband Larry – dead ten years – walked into the post office where I was mailing a package to my son.

Callahan says he spied his first wife and mother of his children, a decade deceased, as he buttered a croissant at a pastry shop on a gray November Thursday. The writer follows this introductory observation with three words: "I'm not crazy."

Through the last ten years I have uttered the same denial to myself over and over and over again. First, after a golden dog appeared out of the blue, no owner insight, at the four-way stop just before my husband's funeral procession turned into the church parking lot. The dog followed the procession the way a loyal companion would follow a long-time master.

I questioned my hold on reality once again after a cardinal seemed to introduce a penetrating song of remembrance on a camping trip six months after Larry's death. After these and other natural events take on a preternatural feel since losing Larry, I have fallen into the habit of, metaphorically, pinching myself. I then force myself to reconsider what has *really* occurred, and weigh the experience by deliberately applying the rote definition of critical thinking passed onto me by a colleague, who attributed it to Vincent Ryan Ruggerio,

Professor Emeritus at the State University of New York. I've used the definition in my classroom for over ten years.

> *Critical thinking is an active mental process in which you scrutinize your ideas or the ideas of others,* (What's going on with this dog or this bird?) *probe their stated and implied meaning* (Are they creatures of this world or another?), *and decide if that meaning is defensible* (How can this be happening?).

The definition continues in my head:

> *Such meaning depends on three characteristics: a questioning attitude to all interpretations or conclusions,* (How can I NOT question these oddities?) *skill in separating fact from opinion and taste from judgment,* (Yes, the dog with no owner did follow the hearse and the bird did precede the song. Am I forcing these events to mean more than they actually do?). Finally I try to keep myself open to *the sensitivity to the connection between ideas.* (Seems like more than coincidence to me).

When this hasty yet deliberate exercise falls short of disproving the uncanny causes and effects I consider, I too say: *I am not crazy.*

The rationale Callahan applies to the appearance of his deceased wife is more complicated. His credentials suggest the complexity of his response to his personal chimera. He is an associate professor of immunology and the public understanding of science in the Department of Microbiology, Immunology, and Pathology at Colorado State University and he holds a joint appointment in the Department of English. Medicine and metaphor combine when, in answer to his encounter with his dead wife, he considers the full ramification of the distinction that only two of our bodies' eleven systems store memories: the immune and nervous systems.

Growing up in the 1950s, a series of Bell Telephone science films hosted by the unassuming Dr. Frank C. Baxter taught me many lessons, including how a nervous system "remembers." Bespectacled

Baxter – introduced in each of his films as Dr. Research – had a flair for explaining complicated science. His easy spin on a process, along with cartoons of the brain as the busy control room of mind-body operations, showed me how the mind and body worked. Touch a hot stove and the animated "nerve people" under our skin push pain buttons that notify our brain to have its people alert the muscle people in our hand to pull away, and the voice people to say, "Ouch." If all systems work - the memory people will keep us away from lit burners in the future.

High school and college biology courses have left me with the basic understanding that if immune systems didn't remember viruses, vaccinations would not work. Too bad Dr. Research is no longer with us (he died in '82) to explain, with cute cartoons and the patience of a scientific saint, the greater complexities of how an immune system remembers. He'd probably start with what Callahan tries to get me to picture when he compares the memory banks of the immune system to Mason jars. Mason jars in which his grandmother and my mother stored all the reusable tidbits of our lives: buttons, buckles, rubber bands, and pennies.

I can follow this analogy for how the immune system stores "intricate things that the rest of the body has forgotten." I understand that "the memories stored inside our immune systems can come back"- like vaccination serums, geared up to fight a recalled toxin. But how can an immune system conjure up a dead spouse? How does it trick me into thinking Larry, buried three miles north on Route 5, just pulled up my driveway in the twilight that eases day into night and reality into abstraction?

Dr. Callahan goes on to explain that, through their relationship – as with any family relationship – his wife had embedded "under his skin" the same way an injected immunization does, via "enveloped viruses – like those that cause colds, flu, cold sores, AIDS." He goes on to inform that these viral host cells contain genetic material along with lipids and proteins.

Some of that DNA or DNA made from RNA clearly gets incorporated into our chromosomes and begins to work inside of us. This means that each time we are infected with one of these viruses, we also acquire a little of the person who infected us, a little piece of someone else. Infection as communication. Infection as chimerization. Infection as memorization.

A few months after my father died, I remember walking up the driveway of his house to visit my mother and thinking, for a moment, that he was sitting on the porch. I could have sworn it was him looking for a garage door spring down an aisle at Home Depot the last time I was there.

I experience something different with Larry. I become conscious of a sense of him (more than the embodiment I perceived with Dad), always when I least expect it. This feeling can occur on an afternoon hike. As I gain speed downhill I am reminded of the double-time pace I once used to match his long strides. He would forge ahead on many a nature walk through Cape Cod marshlands. Six-foot him, five-foot me, I would always find myself huffing and puffing after his steady treads. Now, when I hike alone or with someone else, I'm compelled to lead the way at a high-cardio rate.

Once, on a flight to Los Angeles to visit his brother, the airlines showed a Seinfeld rerun. Larry hooted as loudly as if he were seeing a live stand-up routine. Passengers' heads popped up and turned to catch a glimpse of this merry man who, to them, was so much more entertaining than Jerry, George, and Kramer on screen in front of them. Now, whenever I'm in a theatre, Larry always seems to be hiding somewhere in the dark audience, throwing out his hearty guffaw at the end of a comic show-stopper.

And during those songs of the Seventies I am reminded of a kiss, a touch, the precious terms of endearment and intimacies of our decades together.

According to Dr. Callahan my immune system – with its Mason jar of memories or forget-me-not vaccine – is at work whenever I am unsuspectingly brought to a moment, minute, or milestone in my life with Larry. These recollections are antibodies against the disease of loss.

Or it could be my nervous system, which also plays an unusual role in the bereaved, but in a less understood way than the immune system's storage arrangement.

Here Callahan talks about long-term potentiation (LTP), a means by which certain nerve paths become favored over others. If I could make a call to Dr. Research for the elementary-school-science version of this process, he would no doubt explain how going to the circus and seeing a carful of clowns could bring me back to the experience of Larry walking into my maternity room, carrying a clown lamp for his newborn son. Somewhere between the unloading of six clowns out of a mini-car and tossing a half dozen cream pies into their faces, I find myself recalling the comic figure under the lampshade dressed in baggy yellow and orange harlequin pants as it balances on one leg. Who knew that just attending a Ringling Brother's matinee – with no thought of the past, no thought of the future – would find Larry under the Big Top?

The circus clowns initiated an LTP which connected to the clown on Baby Conor's lamp. That was the easy part of nervous system memory function. Dr. Research always starts with the easy part. I understood the concept for better or for worse. Why else would I have quickly given away the velveteen swivel chair upon which Larry slumped to his death? I could not bear to be reminded of the tragedy to which that piece of furniture connected.

Where the nervous system's role in memory gets more complicated is a crucial area for me or anyone like me -- writing about their past – because it involves the subjective truths of the memories. This is why my memories and my children's memories of the exact same events can be so different.

To get me to understand this, Dr. Research would no doubt ask Emily, Conor, and me to recall the exact date that Larry died. This question calls for a declarative memory that is easy to agree upon: December 8, 1998. No ifs ands or buts with this "explicit, consciously accessible memory," says Callahan. On every anniversary of that date I involuntarily retreat back to the hour by hour horror we experienced the day Larry died. Asked why I was more affected than the children when Eric Clapton's "Tears of Heaven," played as

background music at the funeral home the morning of Larry's buri-
al, and Dr. Research would say that, because I knew the song was
actually written about the untimely death of Clapton's young son
–named Conor, the same as my son's name – the name association
triggered my emotional memory to an even more layered emotional
response to the funeral service than they could imagine. I connected
it to losing their father *and* the loss of a son named Conor. Since
Emily and Conor didn't know the song was written about the tragic
death of someone with the same name as my young son, they would
not experience that layer of meaning.

Emotional memory can also be more subconscious and inacces-
sible. Nothing can fully explain to me why the sight of a Luna
moth seemingly stuck to a window after Emily's eighth grade dance
circuited such a comfort within me, six months after Larry's death.

I'm not sure Dr. Research would even attempt to explain a third
kind of memory to youngsters – at least not the way Dr. Callahan
presents the phenomena. Phantom memory, as in phantom limbs
and phantom hands, "comes from someplace beyond or beneath
declarative and emotional circuits," says Callahan. An amputee often experiences phantom limbs - a sensation that a leg is still there.
Inexplicable by declarative or even emotional memory standards,
the sensation of a phantom limb can also be very painful. Phantom
memory further mystifies the medical community – and me – with
evidence of children born without limbs, who have obviously "never experienced the sensation of a normal limb – (who) experience
phantom limbs." Dr. Callahan continues to explain:

> [The] presence of phantom limbs in these children sug-
> gests that some sort of prenatal image – some template
> of what a human should look like – is formed inside our
> fetal minds before our arms and legs develop. . . before
> even our nervous systems are fully formed. If at birth
> our bodies don't fit this template, our minds say it ought
> to be.

Phantom memories are not limited to limbs. The blind see phantom visions. The deaf, like Beethoven, hear phantom symphonies.

These inexplicable realities raise a key question - especially for a memoir writer: how much of our realities are created inside of our own minds? Scientists do not know. What they do know, according to Callahan, is that "only a tiny portion of our thoughts, are direct results of what we see, hear, taste, smell, or touch. The rest of it, the remainder of our mental imaging, begins and ends inside of us."

Callahan poses a question that hits closer to the heart for the bereaved: If the sudden loss of a limb can be compensated by an imagined limb that feels so real it can hurt - via the complexities of our nervous systems, who is to say that an unexpected loss in our outside world – a loss which interferes with our emotional completeness – might not be compensated, as well, by a "bit of virtual reality that reconciles our world and the real world?"

A friend of mine, who for years has expressed no belief in God, shared a surprising story with me, after I told him about repeated senses of Larry's presence. He too had felt, a number of times, the company of his deceased father, as he walked into an empty room, almost certain the dead man was seated on a nearby rocking chair. And, he felt comforted by this premonition. After reading "Chimera," his experience, along with the sense of Larry's presence in nature (the dolphin, dog, and cardinal) and gesture (the pose of a thumb or an eyebrow) resonate with more understanding than awe. Whether or not there are supernatural ramifications, I may just have been vaccinated against the loss by the intimacies of the man I loved and lost; and, his loss, sudden as it was, may very well hurt as much as it does by nature of him simply not being where he should be – like a phantom limb. Like Callahan I can say I am not crazy. I am just beginning to understand.

FULL OF GRACE

March 31, 2010

Father Kerwan celebrates my mother's funeral Mass - almost twenty years to the day he celebrated my father's Mass for the Dead. At 92, he walks and talks slower but, as a friend remarked after Father spoke about Mom –and Dad – it was as if he was talking to us from a comfortable living room chair. At 60, grieving over Mom's death, I still seek comfort for the loss of my father and husband in Father Kerwan's words.

Jim and Delia.

Father articulates my mother's name with my father's as if it were a one word *halleluiah.* He recalls the early days of the parish when Mom and Dad brought my brother and me to Sunday Mass at the local high school while the church was being built. Larry's family attended then too. He and his brother played on the Holy Family CYO basketball team. In their first year, they won the Northern Deanery Championship.

Father Kerwan became close to our parents - the Haydens of Springfield and the Baiones from Brooklyn. We were two families of hard-working stock, mine first generation American and his, second. Both followed their dream, in the late Fifties, to the same unstoppable development of brand new houses – close to 4000 in ten years – that   created the need for a fourth Catholic parish in town.

Father married Larry and me. Our children received their sacraments from his hands. When Larry died in 1998, the illumination of Father's faith seemed to dull a bit. Father would shake his head and say to me, "This. . . this, I do not understand," a truly holy man revealing that doubt is the cornerstone of faith. Belief, by its nature, belies certainty. I never sought a spiritual answer for why Larry died. Why I was left to live my life without him. If Larry's death baffled Father, I wasn't going to be the one to figure it out.

In her younger days my mother exuded classic 1940s beauty: Full lipstick-lined mouth, penetrating brown eyes accented by thick lashes and prominent eyebrows, long, soft, side-parted hair. She was smart too. Mom skipped a grade for her exceptional schoolwork and graduated from high school early. Then she began working – at sixteen – as a secretary for a shipping company located on the New York City harbor. Her petite frame looked more sophisticated dressed in the padded-shoulders and cinched-waist fashions of the working girl. When she posed for a camera in a halter and tap-dancing shorts, Mom looked like a wholesome pin-up.

A New York artist who was a family friend asked to paint my mother's wedding portrait. White pigment stroked and dotted over pink and gray oils replicate the dainty patterns of lace on the soft, deeply scooped neckline of her gown. Just above the lace, see-through toile rises to the neck. From afar, she appears sensuous. Up close-more demure.

As a Fifties housewife and mother of young twins, she didn't wear the shirtwaist dress and heels TV moms donned as everyday wear. She wore clothes she could cook and clean in. She went without the make-up. But on the few occasions she and Dad would go out on the town – *va va va voom*!

Delia and Jim

Father says their names together again. It reminds me of how I would always think of Jim and Della in the story "The Gift of the Magi" when I heard *Jim and Delia* - identical except for one letter. The similarity didn't end there. O'Henry's couple, poor New Yorkers, lived in the same kind of flats that surrounded my grandfather's barber shop on the old Bowery, downtown.

In the story, the struggling husband sells his most prized possession, a gold watch from his father, to purchase his wife's Christmas present - combs of tortoiseshell and jewels to adorn her beautiful,

knee-length hair. Della, whose eyes still retained their brilliant sparkle, sells her crowning glory to a wigmaker to purchase a suitable
fob for the watch.

From the first time I read that story I have pictured my parents,
in similar circumstances, making the same sacrifices. And I'm sure
that, like the O'Henry couple, they would have shrugged away the
tale's bittersweet twist. After Jim unwraps the fob, he tumbles down
on the couch, puts his hands under the back of his head and smiles.
Della remarks, "My hair grows so fast, Jim!"

October 26, 1962

I am thirteen years old today. I overhear one side of a long distance telephone conversation Mom has with her sister in Brooklyn.
She is crying softly. Her voice quivers.

"It's worse for you, Lee. Being in New York."

Mom hangs up. Then picks up the receiver again and dials her
sister Fran in New Jersey. She sounds just as upset. Fran doesn't live
in New York, but she can see the Empire State Building at the end
of her street.

On the same day – my first day as a teenager – President Kennedy
spends 10 minutes on the White House phone with British Prime
Minister Harold Macmillan. They discuss ultimatums to convince
the Soviets to remove missiles the Russians have placed in Cuba.
Kennedy has already imposed a ship quarantine of this small island
just 112 miles off the Florida coast.

Twenty miles closer than Mom is to Fran.

Soviet Prime Minister Khrushchev doesn't budge. Kennedy tells
Macmillan:

> If, in the end of 48 hours we are getting no place and
> the missile sites continue to be constructed, then we are
> going to be faced with some hard decisions.

Mom doesn't even hang up the receiver. She just clicks the switch
hook before she dials her brother in Staten Island.

We survive the Cuban Missile Crisis. In a few days all is right in the wide world but not in my newly embraced adolescent world. I've been in the bathroom a half hour. A sharp tightness in my stomach finally releases but then squeezes again. I am doubled over, rolled in the protective crouch we practiced in school in a windowless hallway lined with lockers. An area that would protect us through a bombing attack. But my eruptions are internal. And there is blood in the toilet.

A booklet slides under the bathroom door. When I fully extend my arm away from the ball I have rolled myself into, I can reach it. Pick it up. Stare at the cover that mocks my terror. An array of stars surrounds a flat illustration of a pretty girl in a pony-tail and wispy brunette bangs. She stares back at me – her bright saucer eyes gleam above a pug nose and sliver of a smile. And just below this portrait – stylized for the 50s more than the 60s – a title announces *now you are 10*.

"It's OK - just read the book," Mom says from the other side of the door.

Jim and Delia

Father Kerwan relished the stories my Dad used to tell. One he found particularly amusing was how my Dad's brother, a Brooklyn limousine driver who always seemed to be in some sort of pickle, approached our Connecticut home on his first visit, following a police car.

Uncle Joe got out of his car and put his hand through the cruiser's rolled down window to pat the officer on his back. A gesture of gratitude. He had gotten lost on the last lap of the trip, pulled up alongside of the police car, and asked for help. As the man-in-blue drove off, my uncle turned, took a swift look at the open breezeway that connected the house to the garage of our new home, and said, "Nice wind-passer you got there."

I think it was the word "wind-passer" that just broke Father up. His face would redden as he gasped through a laugh so hearty, it interrupted his breathing. When he could talk again he'd say, "That's a good one, Jim."

Mom never saw the humor in the story. Yet, she could laugh at herself, especially in the oft-told dandelion tale, another Father Kerwan favorite. Here we were a family fresh from the Big City and Mom goes to the local garden center to ask for "seeds for those little yellow flowers on everybody's lawn."

"You didn't know they were weeds, Dee," Father would say – a statement, not a question – and then chuckle over her naiveté.

Now, when I think about it, for a girl in her late teens who took the train into the city to work every day, she was pretty naïve. There was never any talk about a boyfriend before Dad. There were family jokes about how, if Dad hadn't come along, she could have been Nicky the Egg Man's bride. Really! I always got the feeling it would have been an Old Italian arranged marriage.

When my brother and I were toddlers, Nicky used to come by our four-family house in Brooklyn every week or so, selling eggs from his chicken farm in New Jersey. The love seat in the living room would have made a comfortable single chair for him. Mom said we were related in some distant fourth-cousin-twice-removed sort of way. Yet, I'd pick up on those innuendos about "if not Dad – Nicky." I never knew if they were true or not.

Jim and Delia

I knew Dad had a girl friend before he met my mother. Mom would bristle at her name: Felicia. It came up now and then because my father had an aunt by the same name. Dad would say, "Not *that* Felicia," and laugh a little. I don't think it was a huge part of his past. People don't usually joke about the really big skeletons in their closets.

I loved the part of Mom and Dad's story I knew was true. They met, were engaged within months, and wed shortly after, on February 15. That doesn't happen much anymore. The date was as close to Valentine's Day as they could arrange a Saturday nuptial.

So I think Mom was naïve about dating and maybe girl relationships too. Not sister relationships. The three sisters had always been very close - and very nervous. Fran has told me how they use to go to the movies together. I can picture her, the youngest, with Lee and Mom, the light from the screen flickering on their faces during a matinee showing of *Since You Went Away*. They'd be mesmerized as they'd watch Claudette Colbert, a beauty they got their 1940s fashion sense from. The actress would capture their hearts playing the war bride, working a man's factory job, taking in boarders, and raising her children alone while her husband fought on the front lines of World War II. Then, Fran has told me, Lee would place two fingers atop her wrist to feel for her pulse. When, between the darkness in the theatre and the loudness of the film, she wouldn't be able to detect the beat, she would run out of the theater afraid she was dying. The other two sisters would follow.

I never knew Mom to have many girly girl friends. She didn't act like a girly girl. She was more a somewhat intimidated immigrants' daughter. If she had to rank relationships, family would be on the top of her list, then Italians, then New Yorkers, and then New Yorkers who moved to Connecticut. This didn't leave much room for Nutmeg State natives. She really liked you if you were an Italian-American New Yorker who moved to Connecticut, especially if you missed your family back in the Big Apple.

Mom always said I was the first in the family to lose my New York accent after the move. It was her way of saying I assimilated better. I didn't feel like a fish out of water, like her; I had just swum upstream a bit and the river felt fine. I always thought her distrust of new friendships might have been a first generation immigrant trait. She also wasn't keen on me going to girly pajama parties and dating. Boys were bad.

1970

> Mothers are much like roses
> A bit thorny but beautiful

April 1990

When a neighbor asked my mother how she managed to put out only one trash can a week, Mom replied, "We eat our garbage." She often spoke with the same succinctness she appreciated when Father said, "Assume a prayerful position," because there were no kneelers in the auditorium where Mass was held. The same no muss, no fuss quality rings out in Della's, "My hair grows so fast," resignation. The same sparseness as in my mother's declaration, "You grew another headlight," whenever I'd wake up with a fresh blemish on my brow. Mom had no need for superfluous goods or words and she took on the risk of having her pithiness misconstrued.

The neighbor's question and Mom's retort appeared in an op-ed piece I wrote for *The Hartford Courant* commemorating the first Earth Day in the spring of 1990. The wires picked up the essay overnight. Three months later *The American Spectator* magazine ran an impudent take on the quote which it had retrieved from a *San Jose Mercury News* reprint.

The American Spectator excerpted the question "How do you manage to have so little garbage?" and Mom's answer about eating it. Then the *Spectator* remarked, "God knows why" someone would report such a thing, that someone being me.

More savvy readers interpreted Mom's 1960s reply as a forerunner of the yet unnamed *green* movement. The full op-ed further explained how Mom made fresh pasta – from flour and eggs – so she didn't accumulate the packaging paper and cardboard that makes up the bulk of household trash. She didn't throw out leftovers, using them instead in casseroles and soups. The vegetables in her minestrone were not dehydrated or stored in cans. Full meals were not frozen inside cardboard and plastic containers that weighed as much as the edible contents. The little cardboard she did accumulate was smashed by an efficient, low-energy compactor – her foot.

A waste-not, want-not woman - my mom. A penny-saver, like Della in the story.

March 28, 1990

Dad dies. Deep inside, all of us knew what lay ahead for my father the afternoon the doctor diagnosed his lung cancer, six months earlier. Yet, he drove straight to my house with Mom that day, sat on the family room couch and said, "I've had a good life." His American Dream come true. I use to think he would have liked to go out more, fine dine, travel a bit. Mom was a real homebody. But he didn't miss the high life any more than Jim missed Della's long hair.

For Dad, Mom had sacrificed living in New York without complaint. But she would never reconcile that she lived to see her daughter became a widow too.

January, 2005

I try to get Mom to go see her brother who is gravely ill in a Staten Island Hospital. She puts off the trip until the funeral. She seems more shaken when we return home from his services. She gazes afar sometimes. Forgets food on the stove. Her doctor tells me to take her car keys. I replace them with a Lifeline emergency alert bracelet.

August, 25, 2005

Che corragio
Alfonso and Carmela
Bore from village to port
Across the Atlantic to
The New World
Where he, a bootblack.
Would tip his hat to the
Copper Lady by day
And hum
America the Beautiful
To Lee, Dee, Fran, and Vin
Each night.

What courage
Delia and Jim
Carried on to Connecticut
Where suburban legend
Sprouted the day
She, the New Yorker, asked
A bemused New England landscaper
For seeds to what he deemed

A yellow weed.

With an immigrants'
   daughter's grit
Delia nurtured
   the twins,
And tended the grandchildren six
Who have brought forth the
great-grandchildren three
As her perpetual garden grows and grows.

Happy 80th Birthday Grammy

April 2006

Lee dies. Her daughter comments that Mom looked distracted at the services, less distraught than one would think. Disconnected. The doctor orders Mom an antidepressant.

May, 2006

Mom tells me there were strangers in her house overnight, the same ones who come to party every night after she has gone to bed. She knows this because, when she gets up in the morning, the TV is still on. "They never turn it off before they leave," she says. The doctor recommends a psychoneurologist. The earliest available appointment is in six weeks.

June 10, 2006

I am summoned to the office at the high school where I teach. My mother's neighbor is on the phone.

The unexpected call floods my mind with fear as I head to the office in a half-run. Eight years earlier the office directive drew me to news of my father-in-law's fatal heart attack. Six months later Larry called to tell me he had been ordered to go to the hospital after a routine stress test. Emily called last year, after she had dialed 911 for herself. I reach the office and beeline to the telephone.

"Laura. There's something wrong with your mother. You need to come," says her neighbor.

"Did she have a heart attack? Did you call an ambulance?" I ask.

"I don't think she needs an ambulance. Just come."

I can see Mom sitting at the table in her double garage as I pull into the driveway. Her neighbor has been keeping an eye on her from across the street. The neighbor meets me at my car door.

"I found her in the middle of the road. She thinks there are men in the house with guns. I got her to go sit in the garage. That's when I went back home and called you."

I coax Mom into the house. Heat up the chicken I brought her the day before. Get her to eat a few bites. Then I call my brother.

"Mom's seeing things. She's saying the stool in the den is a baby crawling and crying. I'm bringing her to Emergency." He takes the Mass Pike two hours west to meet us there.

Mom never goes home again. She requires round-the-clock care and frequent change in the medications that help control the hallucinations. Because she is over eighty and confused, many – family and friends – refer to her as an Alzheimer's patient.

January, 2009

I cut out this news clipping and make copies for whoever asks me how Mom's Alzheimer's is:

Rare case of dementia leaves woman speechless
By PETER GOTT, M.D. Newspaper Enterprise Association

Dear Dr. Gott: My 63-year-old daughter was a healthy, active woman until two years ago, when she started having trouble with her speech. She was diagnosed with frontotemporal dementia (primary progressive aphasia).

Can you tell me what causes this? Is it terminal? Her doctors have said there is no cure.

Dear Reader: Frontotemporal dementia (FTD) is a blanket term for a group of rare disorders that affect the frontal and temporal portions of the brain. Disorders in the group include Pick's disease, primary progressive aphasia and semantic dementia. There is a debate whether to include corticobasal degeneration and progressive supranuclear palsy. Should this happen, the name would likely be changed to Pick Complex.

There is no treatment that has been shown to slow FTD. Behavioral modification, antidepressants and sedative/tranquilizers to control dangerous or unacceptable behaviors may be necessary. Primary progressive aphasia, which your daughter has, affects not only spoken language but written language, as well. Speech therapy may be an option.

Unfortunately, at this time, FTD does appear to be a terminal affliction. Some sufferers may live only two years and others up to 10. Eventually, most will require 24-hour care and monitoring. The rate of deterioration varies.

After they read the article I tell them frontotemporal dementia makes Alzheimer's look like a common cold.

September 2009

Fran and her husband Ralph visit Mom in the high care wing of an assisted living facility. Fran rushes to her, wraps her arms around her shoulders and sobs, "Oooo Delia, how did this happen?" Mom rolls her eyes. She cannot speak, but there are signs that, deep inside that complex brain of hers, she knows exactly what is going on. The brain that got her through high school quicker than the rest, the brain that figured out how to raise two infants at once, recycle before it became a national mandate, and cook so healthfully for my father that he barely lost any weight through his illness - that brain was aware of its limitations. I could see the torment of this awareness in her eyes. The part of the brain that worked was silently shouting, "Get me out of here."

Fran is disappointed she does not get more reaction from Mom, but when she leaves she says, "I feel as if I've visited the Queen."

Delia and Jim

Father stands before us. As I watch him I realize this man who once stood tall above my parents would have to look up to them today. He steadies himself.

"Delia shared much joy with us, but life was not the same without her beloved Jim."

Through the decades Father's posture had taken on the shape of a question mark. He shifts his weight to find a different center of gravity than he had years ago. A more difficult one to find.

"But Delia had her children, grandchildren, and great grandchildren to love and love her." He accents each generation as he looks toward us in the front pews. "And Delia bore her crosses, her loss, her illness," Father shakes his head a moment and seems to have to catch his breath before he exclaims "What grace." Then louder, "Yes, with such grace."

My brother plays "My Mother's Eyes" on an acoustic guitar before the recessional. No one needs to hear the words as he loses himself in the melody, as if he is performing for an audience of one.

NOT READY FOR PRIME TIME HUMOURS

I love Jay Leno, but not because he tells great jokes. Letterman's gags usually top his repartee. Like in their birthday shout-outs to Obama, earlier this year.

Leno: If you want to get him a present, he's registered at Bed, Bath, and Blame Bush.

Letterman: He'll be 49 years old. Yea right, if he had a birth certificate.

Give me subtle over obvious any late night.

It's Leno's profile that sends me - his chin to be exact. That chin of his, before the Tonight Show gig, when he made the cover of *People* magazine in '87, is the same chin that man of mine had. When Larry was in college his roommate drew a two-inch caricature of him: One-third head, two-thirds chin angling down from his jaw to the tip of his stick-figure feet. Jutting, all right. So much so that when the "anvil-faced" comedian, as *People* dubbed Jay, took over for Carson in '92, friends urged Larry, "Send your picture to Leno, maybe you'll get invited on the show."

How protruding was Larry's chin?

So protruding that if that man of mine had made it past his 49th birthday, had lived long enough to send NBC that picture (making him an even more prime target for Leno-look-alike jokes, the way Obama – at 49 – is a prime target for birth certificate jokes) that chin of his would have had to be broken. That's right, intentionally

113

cracked and reset by a guy who cracks and resets jaws for a living; so that my man's upper molars would have finally been able to rest upon his lower molars, not slip into a chasm of jaw that thrust his lower mandible forward. All of this breaking and resetting would, of course, have occurred after Larry's would-be guest appearance on the Tonight Show, after his fifteen minutes of fame, jawing with Jay.

But Larry got way more than fifteen minutes of fame, without having to be like anybody else. The day he died, word spread through town so quickly that, by the time I called to pass the tragic news on to my high school principal at four in the afternoon, after my children were back home and after our house had filled with shell-shocked family and friends, the principal had already reported the sorry account at a faculty meeting - two hours earlier. An EMT leak, I suspect. And, before the early December sun had gone down on that dark, dark day, the president of the town soccer association stopped by my home to pay his respects and generously offer to have the sports club cater the meal that would follow Larry's funeral. "It's the least we can do," he said as I nodded the way I nodded through countless condolences at Larry's wake, two nights later, like a bobblehead, through hours of sympathies from a line of mourners that looped within the room, through the lobby, and out the funeral home door. One expression of empathy, spoken by a soccer mom whose daughters had been coached by Larry for as long as our daughter and son had played the sport – seven years I'd say – seemed the most fitting. She wrapped me in her arms and whispered, "This sucks" in my ear.

Others were sweet. "Let's get together and bake Christmas cookies next week." I couldn't imagine rolling dough and adding sprinkles to snowmen and angels in seven days, or 7,000.

Maybe Dave Letterman should deliver a Top Ten List of What Not to Say to a Young Widow. I could suggest a few doozies: Please don't say God has a plan or God needed him in heaven. That's one Nasty Almighty that would take a father away from his family in the snap of time it takes to read this sentence – the time it takes for a clot to travel, leg to lung. That's it. Bye-bye. The family show's over. Another one for Dave's list: Don't even think about attesting to the woman's strength by saying, "Better you than me." A widow can really pave the road to hell with that one.

Ba-dum, ching!

Letterman's a lucky guy. He had quintuple bypass surgery a year after Larry died. Six weeks later he returned to his desk on Late Night and featured eight members of his medical team on the show. "They installed an EZ Pass," he joked, though obviously moved by the gift of his regained wellness.

Larry - and 59,999 others – didn't get through the recovery toll booth in the year between his surgery and Letterman's - due to a blood clot traffic jam in his lung. He missed out on the opportunity to read Jay's autobiography, *Leading With My Chin,* which became available just after his death. I'm sure he would have been interested to know that Jay's doctors advised him to have his jaw broken too. I can hear Larry saying, "Leno wouldn't even need a surgeon. Conan O'Brien would do it for free." But Leno says he doesn't want to go through the prolonged healing period with his jaws wired shut. Can you blame him, especially after last year's ordeal?

I, for one, am I'm thrilled that Leno will let his jaw be – even if its nonalignment could lead to chewing issues in his old age, headaches even. As long as Jay keeps his jaw the way it is, I can be reminded of Larry's jaw the way it was, the way it would have been. I'm not alone in the infatuation either. Google "Jay Leno's chin" and you get 245 hits: Young Leno with thick curly hair, thin-face, and a pointy chin; middle-aged Leno with a more stylized pompadour, jaw thicker, more protruding; Leno at sixty, with a silver-grey mane and fleshy jowls. That's what the good life'll do to you.

Funny. I can't even write about late night TV without writing about Larry.

I have been writing about Larry's death for some time now. I tried to write about *my* life – five, ten years – after losing him, and those pieces always reverted back to his passing. Then I tried to write about our lives together before losing him, and those pieces always led up to the loss. I realized, if I was going to write - it was, in one way or another, going to be about Larry's death. Grief becomes its own obsession.

Writing about the obsession, comes from me finally admitting that the day Larry died would spill into part of every day I would live for the rest of my life. And in so doing, I became aware that my father's death (before Larry died) and my mother's death (after) have become part of my every day as well. I think, as we get older, we get filled with our losses.

A year or so before Larry died a dear friend of mine lost her husband. She was an older woman, now also gone, who had been my religious instruction teacher when I was younger and then became a very close colleague after we started teaching high school together. So close, she threw me a bridal shower.

My dear friend and her husband – an English teacher and an engineer – were married for over fifty years. She often told me how, on their many long road trips together, she would look up and admire the clouds while he would look up and admire the telephone poles. On one of those long road trips he suffered a stroke. She lost her loving passenger.

When Larry died, my friend comforted me by telling me her grief was like having a hole in her heart. Not the cliché broken heart (though recent studies indicate a survivor can die of the proverbial broken heart) but a heart with a part of it missing. She never mentioned this when Larry was alive. It was a story the bereaved tells the grieving. The hole-in-the-heart image has stayed with me ever since. An adult or child can literally, have a hole in their heart – a simple congenital heart defect – and still live. I think this is a crucial aspect of the metaphor.

Recently a Connecticut doctor, whose wife and daughters were heinously killed three years ago, spoke after one of the murderers was sentenced to death. The state and – since the verdict – the nation have watched Dr. William Petit and his close relatives endure the trial with dignified, silent anguish. When the doctor did speak publicly, after the sentencing, he was asked if he finally felt some closure now that the judgment was passed. He mulled a bit; this was not part of his planned statement. Then he said, "I don't think there's closure. I think whoever came up with that concept is an imbecile – whoever they are who wrote it the first time."

I think that assessment comes from the doctor side of William Petit – the endocrinologist – and it makes me wonder if he might not share the thinking and theories of Dr. Gerald N Callahan, a professor of immunology at Colorado State University. Callahan has written about how memories of deceased loved ones, affect survivors' immune systems.

I have felt the same disdain towards all sources, from funeral home pamphlets to the self-help books that traditionally pigeonhole the grieving process into five stages: denial, anger, bargaining, depression, and acceptance. Sure these are feelings the grief-stricken experience, but like any complicated process made simple, the model boils down to an incomplete, if not wrong, cultural message. Callahan's essay "Chimera," helped me understand my complex grief much more effectively than the traditional Kubler-Ross model from her 1969 book *On Death and Dying*.

In all fairness, science has begun to catch up with Petit's and my gut feeling. An article that appeared in *The New Yorker* this year reexamines Kubler-Ross's findings. The five stage theory was first meant to be a paradigm for the person facing death, not the one left behind. The dying, *not* the grieving. It was later that Kubler-Ross suggested the stages could be applied to the grieving process too.

The New Yorker article suggests that "the stage theory of grief caught on so quickly because it made loss sound controllable . . . based more on anecdotal observation than empirical evidence." Therein lays the problem. Anecdotes are spoken and shared. Most grief-stricken people I know are pretty tight-lipped about their feelings. They may confide with a family member or friend. I suspect more turn inward than reach out to a support group or counselor. If ever there was a silent majority on an American issue, I think it would be sufferers of loss who don't reach closure, who don't let go, who never stop grieving. Sufferers of loss may loop through the five stages: angry today, accepting tomorrow, or part of tomorrow, until the housecleaning is done, or the sun goes down, or a favorite old movie turns up on TNT. Depression almost always returns around the holidays, until a memory – Aunt Ollie (gone thirteen years) telling her young nephews to stop their rhythmic breathing on a family camping trip – transforms the negative energy to laughter around a Thanksgiving table. For a short while Aunt Ollie's sister, who still aches over Ollie's loss, is sated with remembrance the way turkey and all the trimmings have filled her at the family feast. But then Christmas comes, or Ollie's birthday, or just the sight of her home on Main Street, inhabited by someone else's sister, and the grieving sister slumps again, hungry for Ollie's presence, year after year after year.

After Dr. William Petit called the closure theorists "imbeciles, he said, "And I think many of you know it, (you) who have lost a parent, a child, or a friend. There's never closure. There's a hole. . . it's a hole with jagged edges and over time the edges may smooth out a bit, but the hole in your heart and the hole in your soul is still there." I watched him on my TV, a late-middle-aged widower, and I knew he would continue to hurt and yet continue to survive with a piece of his heart missing.

Perhaps adults who suffer deep loss should be looked at the same as children who suffer loss. When Larry died, books on how to help myself and my children through the tragedy explained that Emily and Conor would first grieve as the eleven and thirteen year-olds they were. Then they would grieve as older teens, then as young adults. No chapters were devoted to how I would start grieving as a 49-year old, then as a woman in my fifties, then in my sixties.

I was one of 700,000 women widowed in 1998. One third of us were under 45. Most of us younger ones lost our husbands suddenly. Most of us were caring for young children. We were not our grandfather's or our father's widows.

My grandmother and mother lost their husbands later in their married lives. Their losses, in their sixties and seventies, were no less painful than mine, but they had other widowed friends to share their losses with. Going back another generation, my great-grandmothers, widowed in the 1940s, would have been expected to become reconciled with their husband's deaths in two months.

Unlike the older bereaved, most young widows have young children to support, comfort, and prepare for a return to school and activities. Many of them, like me when Larry died, work full time, place their children's dinner time, homework time and soccer practices highest in their day's priorities, and are too exhausted to seek out a support group - probably overpopulated with older widows anyway.

Perhaps, no young widow is *not* an island. Very few of my coupled friends could relate to the everyday loneliness of my loss through the years. They may have sympathized, but they could not empathize. Most of them wanted me to hurry up and get better. For my sake? Maybe. Yet, they acted as if grief was contagious. They didn't want to get too close - less they contract it. Whether they knew it or not, a few of my new millennium friends were going by the 1940s model, setting an eight-week limit on my grieving. Most of the others shared the expectation reported in a 1989 article in *The Washington Post* - that 85 % of young widows mull over their loss for four to seven years.

Now, over twenty years later, even that timetable has come into question. Researchers are coming closer to what the bereaved already know. Loss changes lives too drastically to expect its sufferers to "get over it." I can't come to *accept* my husband died any more than I can *accept* that over 3000 Americans perished on September 11, 2001, or *accept* that over half that number did not survive Hurricane Katrina. But I can work through these private and public pains. *Work through* as in *function,* not as in *now you feel it, now you don't.* Of course the sorrow is more difficult to work through when the tragedy is personal but, as *The New Yorker* article brings out, humans are programmed to grieve, just the way the dolphins Larry and I watched off the shore of California were instinctively designed to lead the remains of their kind through a ritual of mourning.

If then, by our nature, we humans are designed to grieve, so too are most of us hardwired to function through the sadness. George A. Bonanno, a clinical psychologist at Columbia University, calls this quality "resilience" in his book *The Other Side of Sadness: What the New Science of Bereavement Tells Us about Life after Loss,* published last year. My daughter, son, and I did not look forward to facing each day without Larry, but each of us, eventually, did look forward. Even with a hole in each of our hearts.

This brings me back to metaphor - and to writing about Larry. When I started to put Larry's story on the page – the only story I could put on the page at the time – all I could write was metaphor. How did I feel? Like these dolphins I saw in California. What did I use to express my grief? A camping story about an encounter with a flaming red bird. I was connecting to nature more than to people. Wild life, ocean life, these creatures knew more about mortality than anybody I knew – or so I thought. Then, over a period of time, my old friend told me about the hole in her heart. Another woman I am close to told me about Papa's Day, her father's same birth and death date anniversary, which happened to also land on Veterans Day. He was a World War II vet. Someone else shared how he once thought he saw his dead father rocking in his favorite chair. Another, about how he raised his daughter alone after her mother died. Stories of loss engendered more stories of loss. One after the other - until, lo and behold, my best high school friend shared her dream about Larry with me, and my God (I use that exclamation for all its worth) something changed. I wrote down everything everybody told me, discovering more and more about Larry's death every time I put pen to paper, just as with this surprising burst of perception.

As I learned to listen more carefully to other people and let their stories of loss lead me to discover what I had to say, something else happened. The story I was hellbent on writing about Larry became a story about me. I didn't plan it that way, but then, since Larry died, I've learned not to plan on a whole lot of things.

Eventually someone read one of my stories - the one where I kept asking myself *where was Larry when I needed him?* and then found out. Afterwards she took me aside to tell me her mother had been a widow for a very long time, and that she never really understood her mother - until she read my story. Just as I was trying to wrap my head around that, someone else read all my stories and told me that they sounded like they were about a strong, independent, and spiritual woman.

You could have fooled me.

Now, I'm doing the fooling – with all this Leno and Letterman stuff. But the fooling feels right. And I know if Larry could read what I've written, "Not Ready for Prime Time Humours" would be his favorite piece. Because it takes something we can't control – death – and tries to lasso it with some things we can. Our resilience. Our reclamation of spirit. Our good humor.

Recently political raconteur Jon Stewart told America that "sometimes the light at the end of the tunnel isn't the Promised Land. Sometimes it's only New Jersey." What a hoot and yet, what truth rests in that line. In an interview with the President, Stewart even got Obama to say he stood for "Change we can believe in – *but*." LMAO, as we say on Facebook to those who share our statuses and stories.

Laughing won't bring Larry back. Laughing doesn't decrease the deficit or lessen the number of soldiers who gave their lives in Iran or Afghanistan. But it gets us through to the next crisis.

After 911, one of the surest signs that New York City was going to be okay was the first live broadcast of *Saturday Night Live,* 18 days after the attack. New York Mayor Rudolph Guiliani opened the show by paying tribute to the lives lost on September 11th and acknowledging the members of the New York Fire and Police Departments as heroes. My heart swelled as Paul Simon sang the words "but the fighter still remains," from his seventies song "The Boxer."

Then guest host Reese Witherspoon told an off color joke. A long story about a baby polar bear who kept asking Mama and Papa Polar Bear if he really was a polar bear, over and over and over again until Mama Polar Bear said, "But why do you keep asking me that?"

The baby polar bear replied, "Because I'm freezing my balls off!" Lorne Michaels, the show's creator, wanted her to say "Because I'm freezing my *fucking* balls off." He had already told her he would pay the FCC indecency fine "just so he could prove to viewers that New York City was back up and running." Witherspoon chickened out.

When Weekend Update rolled around, Tina Fey brought the viewers up to SNL news-tampering standard when she told a story about a North Carolina man who owned a Middle-Eastern restaurant named Osama's Place. She reported the true news - that he wouldn't change the name since it was named for the original owner, not Osama Bin Laden. "Still," she continued, as straight-faced as any prime-time news anchor, "He had a harder time explaining why his other restaurant was named 'Hitler's Chicken'."

There's something to be said for comic relief.

GROUNDED

Fifty years ago, my mother asked the manager of the Enfield Garden Center for the seeds for "those little yellow flowers on everybody's lawn." We had transplanted our Brooklyn roots to northern Connecticut. What did any of us know about dandelions, the scourge of every suburbanite's lawn?

In Brooklyn, anything that grew through sidewalk cracks was revered. Backyard gardens cramped a few tomato plants, a row of lettuce leaves, and a row of radishes together, in about half the space seeding instructions recommended.

The lushest spot on the block was the corner fruit and vegetable stand. Baskets of beans, bananas, apples, and artichokes slanted towards short women in housecoats who had a knack for squeezing and snapping the produce for freshness.

Grandma wore one of those housecoats. She also knew more about dandelions than any of us. In Italy her mother would serve the green –sometimes raw, sometimes cooked.

A few months after we moved, Grandma and Grandpa traveled to Enfield from Brooklyn to visit us in what they called "the country." Grandpa, a barber, first snipped his son's and grandson's overgrown hair out on our undergrown lawn. A lawn blighted with a yellow flower here, a yellow flower there. Then we all headed to the Warehouse Point Trolley Museum.

Grandma would wait out the nostalgic ride seated on the webbed lawn chair Dad kept in our '55 Plymouth, or so we thought. By the time we got back to her, she had filled the car's trunk with jagged dandelion leaves.

More comfortable with Italian than English, she called the bounty, "*Cicoria,*" Mom and Grandma washed the leaves and prepared
one full, macaroni pot a day through her week-long visit. Steamed,
the bounty shrunk, resembling seaweed. And, how the taste of those
toothy greens did bite, like the lion's teeth for which the leaves are
named.

I find myself a third-generation dandelion lover. It 's never been
for the taste, but more for the sunny bouquets my preschool daughter would pick and offer saying, "These are for you, Mommy," or
the sight of my five-year-old son's puffed cheeks as he prepared to
send a matured fluff ball of seeds into the air. Some of the tiny para-
chutes of white down would settle a short distance away from the
parent plant; others would float out of sight.

One spring it occurred to me that a dandelion seed's flight was
not so unlike my grandfather's ocean voyage across the Atlantic.
My father's account of his family's history immortalized how his
father – as a six-year-old in the early 1900s – held fast to his older
brother with one hand and, with the other, waved good-bye to his
parents who remained rooted to the rocky Italian soil. From Old
World poverty to New World promise they sent their youngest son
across the ocean at a great price – never to see him again.

I also wonder about how this new land inspired another Italian
immigrant – my mother's father – to give each of his four children a
nickel every time he heard them sing *God Bless America.* Something
assured him, through the hardship of departure and obstacles of as-
similation, that his trip would improve his life and provide descen-
dants like me with opportunities he never had.

By the time my mother's father, a shoe-shiner, sailed back to Italy
to see his mother, thirty years later, his wife had died. I have no real
recollection of her, except for a family photo taken at my parents'
wedding. Ten years older than Grandpa, she looks serious, even
stern, as she stands between my mother-the-bride and Grandpa.
The father and daughter are smiling. Judging by all of their faces,
Grandma's life was harder than his.

When Grandpa returned to his mother in Quaglietta, a tiny town
just southeast of Naples, his two-way ticket entitled him to tourist

class, an upgrade from the steerage quarters he, his pregnant wife, and his baby endured on their trip to America, three decades earlier. In a home movie of his departure, he waves goodbye as proudly as the captain of any ship.

On the high seas to Italy he passed his younger brother immigrating to America on a west-bound liner - the SS Andrea Doria. The foggy night before his brother's ship was scheduled to sail into Ellis Island, it approached Nantucket. According to one source, just as "the dance band in the first-class Belvedere Room nightclub had launched into yet another rendition of 'Arrividerci, Roma'," the ship collided with the eastbound MS Stockhom in a maritime disaster that took over fifty lives. My grandfather's brother, along with his wife and three children, survived.

Meanwhile, Grandpa took sick on board his liner, eastbound to Naples. He made it to his mother (who would live to be over 100) a gravely ill man in his fifties. My Uncle Vin, Grandpa's youngest child, flew across the Atlantic to be with his father in the rocky town by a river. Vin wrote three or four letters to Mom about their father's critical days. He ended each correspondence with instruction to "Tell my wife I love her. There's no time to write to more than one person."

I was five years old when my mother received the news of her father's death. There was confusion in the house about a telegram that got waylaid to the outdoor trash before it made it to Mom. Sabotaged by someone who, I suppose, wanted to spare her the news as long as possible. When she finally read it, she moaned deep and sorrowful sounds I had never heard before. Uncle Vin escorted the body back over the Atlantic to America,

I've been told that, at Grandpa's wake, I walked straight to the closed casket, kneeled, and recited the Hail Mary as if I wanted his mother, who remained in Quaglietta, to hear me. A first-grader's first brush with mortality.

The brothers' stories still give me pause. One, a widower, on safe voyage to Naples, gets sick and dies overseas. The other survives a maritime disaster along with his wife and three children. All in the same week. Go figure. I have a hazy memory of my parents, brother, and I going into Manhattan one night, a short time after Grandpa's funeral, to visit the Andrea Doria survivors. They showed us their rope burns.

My mother could not have woken up one morning to find little yellow flowers on her suburban lawn without having borne, well, the ancestral scars of her immigrant past. It doesn't surprise me that she never referred to a dandelion as a weed. Thanks to her, I've always thought the dandelion too pretty and whimsical to be labeled landscape blight. At 60, I still smile at her desire to cultivate the little yellow flowers. Her story's comic edge has smoothed to treasured reminiscence, now that she's gone, along with my father and husband.

I recently moved from Enfield to a neighboring town, so I guess I haven't outgrown my notion of dandelion seedlings' flight either. My daughter is settled with her fiancé, a young man who she tells me grounds her, as her father grounded me, in this unsteady universe. My son, seeking a career in sports management, works hard, plays hard. He wears his independence well. Through every day I am reminded of a seed's natural, inevitable departure from the parent plant and my grandparents' voyages from their mother country. Like Grandma in her housecoat, I add a few of its leaves to a crisp lettuce salad. They've become gourmet. There will be *cicoria* in Em's wedding feast too. Over time I've developed a taste for the bitter green.

BIBLIOGRAPHY

"10 Rules for Dating My Daughter." *Dave's Daily*. 2007, http://www.davesdaily.com/funpages/10_rules_for_dating_my_daughter.htm (accessed August 30, 2010).

Alter, George, Martin Dribe, and Frans Van Poppel. *Widowhood, family size, and post-reproductive mortality: A comparative analysis of three populations in nineteenth-century Europe* [Electronic version].November, 2007. *Demography. 44(4)*, 785-806. http://muse.jhu.edu/login?uri=/journals/demography/v044/44.4alter.html (accessed October 10. 2009).

Armstrong, Alexandra, CFP, CMFC, and Mary R. Donahue, Ph.D. *A Widow's Passage to Emotional & Financial Well Being*, Chicago, Illinois, 2000.

Ballard, Bob. "Andrea Doria." *Lost Liners* pbs.org. 1995-2010. http://www.pbs.org/lostliners/andrea.html (accessed November 6, 2010).

Callahan, Dr. Gerald. N. "Chimera". *In Fact: The Best of Creative Nonfiction*. Ed. Lee Gutkind. New York: W.W. Norton & Company, 2005.

Church of the Holy Family. South Hackensack, NJ: Custombook, Inc. Ecclesiastical Color Publishers, 1969.

"Consegrity." *The Medical Dictionary*. Farlex Inc. 2010. http://medical-dictionary.thefreedictionary.com/consegrity (accessed July 25, 2010).

Didion, Joan. *The Year of Magical Thinking*. New York: Random House, 2005.

Dorkin, Rhoda. "Facing Life Alone Again : Loss of a Spouse at a Young Age Leaves Many People Without Emotional Support" [Electronic version]. *The Washington Post (Health Focus)*, 10 January 1989, http://www.havenofnova.org/

articles/widow_widowers_grief/facing_life_alone_again.
pdf (accessed October 10, 2009).

"Dr. Petit Speaks to Press.".*The Hartford Courant* website, courant.
com. Online available November8, 2010, http://www.
courant.com/community/cheshire/cheshire-home-invasion/
hc-hayes-verdict-death-penalty-20101108,0,6875785.story
(accessed November 11, 2010).

Enfield, CT (Connecticut) Houses and Residents 2010, http://www.
city-data.com/housing/houses-Enfield-Connecticut.html
(accessed November 10, 2010).

Gott, Peter. M.D. "Rare Dementia Leaves Patient Speechless," *The
Hartford Courant,* December 16, 2008.

Hayden, Laura. "I Was a Middle-Aged V-BAC." *New York Family.*
May, 1993, p. 32. "When Birthing's Better the Second Time
Around." *Connecticut Parent Magazine.* January, 1989, p.
5+.

Jamison, Kay Redfield. *Nothing Was the Same: A Memoir.* New
York: Alfred A. Knopf, 2009.

Lieberman, Morton, Phd. *Doors Close, Doors Open: Widows,
Grieving and Growing.* New York: G.D. Putnam's Sons,
1996.

Miller, Sally Downham, Ph.D. *A memoir of grief and recovery.*
Deerfield Beach, Florida: Health Communications, Inc.,
1999.

Myers, Donna. *Cancer Memoirs. About.com. online available,
August 12, 2007,* http://coloncancer.about.com/od/thebasics/
tp/CancerMemoirs.htm (accessed August 25, 2007.

"Pulmonary Embolism." *A to Z topics: health and disease
information.* PennState Milton S. Hersey Medical Center
College of Medicine, updated 31 October 2006, http://www.
hmc.psu.edu/healthinfo/e/embolism.htm (accessed August
25, 2010).

"Pulmonary Embolism." *Medpedia.* Medpedia Incorporated, 2007-
2010, http://wiki.medpedia.com/Pulmonary_Embolism
(accessed August 25,2010).

Ramel, Gordon. "Bird Sounds" Earth – Life Web Productions, September 9, 2008, http://www.earthlife.net/birds/song.html (accessed January 19, 2009).

Rufus, Anneli. *The Farewell Chronicles: How We Really Respond to Death.* New York: Marlowe & Company, 2005.

Salamon, Maureen. *Profiles in Heart Disease: David Letterman.* About.com: Heart Health Center, 31 December 2009, http://heartdisease.about.com/lw/Health-Medicine/Conditions-and-diseases/Profiles-in-Heart-Disease-David-Letterman.htm (accessed Retrieved August 25, 2010).

Saturday Night Live Transcripts, "09/29/01: "Reese Witherspoon / Alicia Keys" http://snltranscripts.jt.org/01/01a.phtml, (accessed November 12, 2010).

Schiff, Harriet Sarnoff. *The Bereaved Parent.* New York: Penguin Books, 1978.

Sherwood, Ben. "What it Takes to Survive. " *Newsweek.* (Online), 2 Feb 2009, http://www.newsweek.com/id/181290 (accessed February 14, 2009).

Sontag, Susan. *Illness as Metaphor and Aids and its Metaphors.* New York: Farrar, Straus and Giroux, 1978.

Tambling, Richard. "Lucky Limericks." *Journal Inquirer.* March 17, 1987

"Vicky Kennedy's First Interview Since Senator Ted Kennedy's Death."The Oprah Winfrey Show. CBS, Harpo Productions, Chicago, IL, 25 Nov. 2009.

widowsbridge.com."Widow statistics." *Loss, grief and renewal (blog),* 6 January 2008, http://ajourneywelltaken.blogspot.com/2008/01/widow-statistics.html (accessed October 29, 2009).

Williamson, Mike. "Subject: Dolphin refuses any aid while (fwd)." online available WhaleNet Archive, 3 June 1997, http://whale.wheelock.edu/archives/whalenet97/0283.html (accessed August 20, 2010).

Woolf, Virginia. *On Being Ill.* Ashfield, Massachusetts: Paris Press, 2002. *Selected Essays.* New York: Oxford University Press. 2008.

ABOUT THE AUTHOR

Laura spent her childhood in Brooklyn, NY, and her teens in Enfield, CT, where she went on to teach high school and freelance for regional publications. She married, raised her daughter and son through her thirties and forties, and was widowed before she turned fifty. She completed her MFA in Writing at Western Connecticut State University in 2010.

Laura's previous writing has been published by *The Hartford Courant*, *Northeast* magazine, the *Journal Inquirer*, *Connecticut Parent*, *Hartford Woman*, and *Imprint* publications . Her essay, "Saved by the Belle" took first place in the *First Annual Mark Twain Days Essay Contest on American Politics & Government*, judged by Russell Baker, Garry Trudeau, and Joyce Chadwick-Joshua. Recently, her essay "Nesting" received an honorable mention from *Connecticut Review*, a journal published by the Connecticut State University system.

TESTIMONIALS

In her luminous memoir, *Staying Alive: A Love Story,* Laura B. Hayden shares personal observations about loss and grief written after the death of her beloved 49-year-old husband, Larry. Faced with raising two children alone and her own struggle with cancer, Hayden digs deep to tell her poignant story of life reinvented. Her astute observations of the natural world clearly informed her ability to create a totally invested life for herself and her children. Here, they contribute to her inspired and vividly real story of perseverance that speaks to human resilience and the power of love.

Irene Sherlock, author of *Equinox*

With vivid candor, Laura B. Hayden acknowledges the many ways grief overwhelms a young woman as she builds a "new normal" after her husband's untimely death. Leading the reader into her life and the lives of her two children, Laura searches for a reason to make sense of the tragedy. Never with pity, Laura embraces the image of her husband in their children, as they grow into adults. When tragedy strikes again, in the form of cancer, Laura gives the reader another glimpse of faith and strength. Told through her voice, Laura will take you on a journey of love and sorrow, joy and hope, and ultimately the conclusion that our loved ones are never completely gone from us.

Elizabeth F. Szewczyk
author of *My Bags Were Always Packed: A Mother's Journey Through Her Son's Cancer Treatment and Remission*

Laura B. Hayden's memoir is a powerful reflection on the most unimaginable loss a person can suffer--the sudden death of a spouse.

Hayden is a rare author who combines personal maturity, honesty, and wisdom with an excellent writer's sense for how to tell her story in a way that discovers the universal humanity in such a private event. She is able to celebrate the beauty and joy of life while simultaneously plumbing the depths of a great sorrow.

To invoke a cliché that is perfectly apt in the case of Laura B. Hayden's new book, "you'll laugh, you'll cry." Most of all, you'll connect.

John Sheirer

author of *Loop Year*

and

Growing Up Mostly Normal in the Middle of Nowhere

CPSIA information can be obtained at www.ICGtesting.com
Printed in the USA
LVOW060132110112

263312LV00002B/18/P